What Life Was Like®

IN THE LANDS OF THE PROPHET

Islamic World
AD 570 ~ 1405

What Life Was Like

IN THE LANDS OF THE PROPHET

Islamic World
AD 570 ~ 1405

BY THE EDITORS OF TIME-LIFE BOOKS, ALEXANDRIA, VIRGINIA

CONTENTS

In the Lands of the Prophet

ARABIA FELIX– "ARABIA THE BLESSED"

At first glance, the Arabian Peninsula seems an unlikely birthplace for one of the world's great religious, cultural, and political movements. Squeezed between Africa and Asia, it is a hot, parched wedge of land of more than a million square miles, much of it traversed only by nomadic tribesmen, the Bedouin. For the inhabitants of Arabia in the seventh century AD, life passed much as it had for thousands of years, an endless trek from pasture to oasis and back, its rhythm as predictable as the march of time. Largely untouched by changes that swept the rest of the world, the Arabs knew little of the empires of the day.

In the year 633, however, the tribesmen of Arabia were preparing to make their own mark on history. Under the unifying banner of their prophet, Muhammad, Arab warriors burst out of their desert homeland and into the neighboring lands of plenty, driven by the twin promises of booty in this life and paradise in the next.

Syria and Palestine fell to them, then Iraq, Egypt, and Persia, territories all formerly ruled by the region's two great powers, the Byzantine Empire and the Sassanian empire of Persia. Within 100 years, these followers of Muhammad had carved out an empire of their own that stretched from Spain to India. And across this vast realm, five times a day, the faithful were facing the Arabian town of Mecca and praying in Arabic: "There is no god but Allah, and Muhammad is His Prophet."

Who were these people who strode with such boldness from obscurity to the center of the world stage? They traced their ancestry to Abraham, patriarch of both the Jews and the Arabs. According to tradition, Abraham and his family left their home in the Mesopotamian city

ca. 570	610		622	630
Birth of Muhammad	Traditional date of Muhammad's call to the prophethood		The flight of Muhammad and his followers from Mecca to Medina (the Hijra); recognized as the first year of the Muslim Era	Muhammad conquers Mecca

of Ur in the second millennium BC and went to live in Palestine. Convinced she was barren, Sarah, Abraham's wife, persuaded her husband to marry his Egyptian servant, Hagar, who gave birth to a baby boy, Ishmael. Several years later, Sarah bore a son of her own, who was named Isaac. Fearing that first-born Ishmael would overshadow Isaac, Sarah induced Abraham to cast out his second wife and her son.

Abraham is said to have taken Hagar and Ishmael to the vicinity of Mecca, a caravan stop in the mountainous western region of Arabia known as the Hijaz, then returned to Sarah. Soon, Hagar and her son were in desperate straits: The provisions Abraham had left them were disappearing fast, and their water was running low. One day, however, young Ishmael dragged his foot through the sand and up bubbled a spring of clear, cool water. Later the spring would become known as the well of Zamzam, a place of pilgrimage for Muslims. And when

Abraham returned to Mecca to visit Hagar and his eldest son, he and Ishmael built a shrine to the one true God; centuries later it would be revered as Islam's holiest site, the Kaaba.

Eventually, Ishmael married a local woman, and his offspring became known as Arabs, while the children of his half brother, Isaac, became the Israelites. As Ishmael's descendants began to move out beyond Mecca, some made their way down to the highlands at the southern end of the Arabian Peninsula. Conditions in southern Arabia were less harsh than those in the north. The southern lands enjoyed regular summer monsoon rains that provided up to 30 inches of annual rainfall. This precious water was carefully managed by the region's farmers, who caught the runoff in reservoirs and irrigation channels that led to terraced fields on the mountain slopes, where they grew such staples as barley, wheat, melons, and almonds.

Over time, as the farming villages of southern Arabia blossomed, great kingdoms began to form among the

632

Death of Muhammad; Abu Bakr becomes caliph, leader of the Muslim community

633-642

Arab conquest of Syria, Palestine, Iraq, Egypt, and most of Persia

661

Islam splits into rival Sunni and Shiite factions after the assassination of Caliph Ali; the Umayyad dynasty comes to power and makes Damascus capital of the Islamic world

711-714

Muslim forces overrun Spain, which they name Al-Andalus

mountain peaks, kingdoms boasting stone palaces filled with alabaster statues adorned with lapis lazuli and gold. One palace had a roof fashioned from a single slab of marble that was said to be so translucent an observer could distinguish between a kite and a crow flying above. Such prosperity did not come from agriculture alone, however. Another source of wealth arose from the region's propitious location astride a number of important trade routes, upon which the lands of the Mediterranean depended for access to the East. At the southern end of the Red Sea, merchant vessels from the Indian Ocean unloaded gems, spices, textiles, and other goods from India and China. These precious cargoes were then reloaded onto Arabian camel caravans for transport north to cities in Syria and Palestine.

Even more valuable to southern Arabia than any of these luxuries from the East, though, were two local commodities. From the trunks of two of the region's va-

rieties of balsam trees oozed gum resins that were much sought after in ancient times: frankincense and myrrh. These precious resins were used in cosmetics and healing ointments and during various religious rites. The New Testament account of the Three Wise Men, who gave gifts of gold, frankincense, and myrrh to the Christ child, reflects the value of the two products, which ranked with gold, the most precious metal of the day, and were thus appropriate tributes for a newborn king.

Good fortune, it seemed, had smiled on the peoples of southern Arabia. Greek and Roman chroniclers of the first and second centuries AD marveled at the region's riches. With good reason the celebrated geographer and cartographer Ptolemy called the land Arabia Felix— "Arabia the Blessed." The same could not be said of the peninsula's arid interior, however. This was the domain of the Bedouin, the true desert nomads, known to the Greeks as Sarakenoi—"people who dwell in tents."

750

Umayyad dynasty overthrown by the Abbasids, who found the city of Baghdad in 762

909

Beginning of the Fatimid caliphate in North Africa

969

The Fatimid dynasty conquers Egypt and transfers its seat to the new city of Cairo in 973

1096

The First Crusade is launched to recover the Holy Land from the Muslims

Fiercely independent, proud of their skill at arms, the Bedouin looked down their noses at their sedentary oasis cousins but could not have survived without them. The oasis settlements were the desert's gardens and marketplaces, supplying date palms and grain. Some oases were caravan stops, with bazaars where the Bedouin purchased weapons, tools, clothing, and other necessities of desert life. In return, the nomads offered camels, milk, hides, and protection from raiders.

By the middle of the sixth century, three major settlements existed in northern Arabia. All three were located in the mountainous Hijaz, bordered by the Red Sea to the west and the great desert to the east. In the central section of the Hijaz was Yathrib, later renamed Medina, an oasis of farms and villages spread over 20 square miles. Some 250 miles to the south lay Taif, a town in the mountains that was used as a cool summer refuge by wealthy Arabians. Immediately northwest of Taif was Mecca, located about 50 miles inland from the Red Sea and set in a rocky ravine, surrounded by mountains devoid of vegetation. Of these three towns, Mecca was by far the richest and the most important. It was at the crossroads of the lucrative caravan trade and was the site of Arabia's holiest pagan shrine, the Kaaba. It was also the birthplace of the founder of Islam, the prophet Muhammad.

In the chapters ahead we will see just how Muhammad is said to have received his revelation from God, how the first Islamic community was established at Medina, and how that small religious community transformed itself into a mighty political empire. We'll learn why Islam was racked by civil war after the Prophet's death and then split permanently into Sunni and Shiite factions. And we'll see how the message of a humble merchant from Mecca affected the daily life of Spaniards, Moroccans, Egyptians, and others who lived in Dar al-Islam, "the Realm of Islam"—the lands of the Prophet.

1218

Beginning of the Mongol conquests

1236

Spanish Christians conquer Cordoba

1250

Mamluk generals seize power in Egypt

1401

Turkic forces led by Tamerlane sack Damascus

Within a century of their prophet's death, the Muslims of Arabia had completely remade the map of the Middle Eastern and Mediterranean regions. Once on the fringes of civilization, they now ruled a mighty empire that spanned three continents, reaching from the steppes of central Asia and the Indus River valley in the east to the Atlantic coasts of Morocco and Spain in the west. And at a time when Europe was mired in the Dark Ages, the Arab conquerors were building vibrant new cities that became centers of commerce and learning, the most notable being Baghdad, the empire's capital from 762.

The political unity of Islam would not long endure. The unwieldy empire's more far-flung provinces soon became essentially independent of Muhammad's successors, the caliphs, beginning with Spain in the mid-eighth century and followed by Morocco, Algeria, Tunisia, Khurasan in Persia, and Egypt. The caliphs' governmental role effectively ended in the 10th century, when a Persian dynasty established itself as the real power behind what was left of the caliphal throne.

From the 11th century onward, Turks, crusaders, and Mongols held sway over core cities and territories of the former empire. But despite its political fragmentation, the medieval Islamic world maintained a significant degree of cultural cohesion. A 13th-century Spanish Arab visiting Alexandria or even more distant Basra would have found much that was familiar in his new surroundings, including the language, the body of law, and of course, the ritual of praying while bowing in the direction of Mecca.

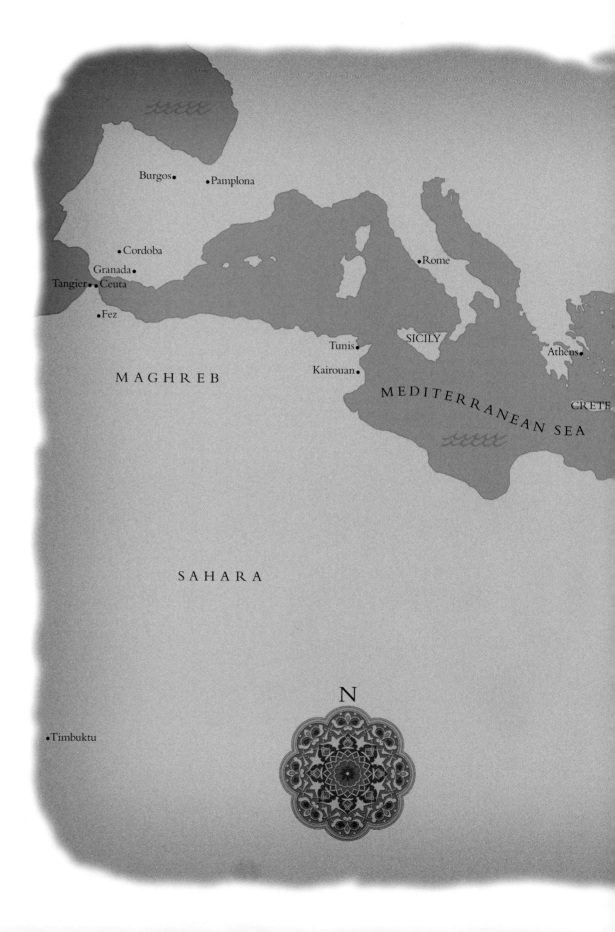

CHAPTER ONE

"THE MESSENGER OF GOD"

Depicted as a herald blowing a trumpet, the archangel Gabriel delivers a message from God to Muhammad. Because God was beyond human perception, he communicated with his prophet only through the archangel. Muslims believe they are attended in their daily lives by two angels, one to record their good deeds, the other to record their bad ones.

According to legend, Muhammad decided to host a dinner to tell his remarkable story. He invited 40 of the most prominent men in his clan to his home, a humble mud-brick structure typical of Mecca's houses, and served them a simple meal of mutton and milk. He knew it was the tradition among Arabs to make an ostentatious show of hospitality to demonstrate the host's wealth and power, but such pretense offended Muhammad. The meal was so modest, in fact, that one of the guests later insisted that it had consisted of only one leg of mutton and one cup of milk that, like Christ's loaves and fishes, miraculously multiplied to feed everyone present. Unlike Christ, however, Muhammad never claimed the power to work miracles. He was, he declared, "a man like other men," a prophet through whom God had chosen to speak. And what he had to say to his guests that evening in AD 615 would change the world.

As his kinsmen finished their meal, Muhammad rose to his feet. They watched him expectantly, and a hush fell over the room. What they saw was a man in his mid-40s, of compact build and average height, with thick, curly hair and beard, sad eyes, and a luminous expression. Muhammad chose his words carefully. "I know of no

Arab," he began, "who has come to his people with a nobler message than mine."

The message, he said, had come to him in a series of divine revelations, the first of which had occurred five years earlier on Mount Hira, not far from Mecca. He'd gone to the mountain, as he'd often done in the past, to meditate. One night, while sheltering in a cave on the mountainside, Muhammad was visited by an apparition. "Muhammad," the figure called out to him. "I am Gabriel and you are the messenger of God. Recite!"

Terrified, Muhammad replied, "What shall I recite?"

"Recite, In the name of thy Lord who created all things . . . " The words dictated by the angel on Mount Hira became what Muslims believe is the oldest passage of the Koran, the sacred text made up of the revelations that God disclosed to Muhammad that night and over the course of the Prophet's life.

Muhammad went on to tell the assembled clansmen of further visions and revelations. Through him the people were commanded to give up idolatrous beliefs and practices and to worship the one universal and all-powerful God, or Allah. To escape divine wrath and eternal damnation, they must pray, give alms to the poor, and above all, surrender themselves to the mercy of God.

Muhammad's message was greeted with derision. After he finished speaking, most of his kinsmen stood up and laughed. Only his 13-year-old cousin Ali declared that he would follow Muhammad. But what Muhammad conveyed to his clan that evening was nothing less than the heart of a new religion that would spread with breathtaking speed. It would become known as Islam, from the Arabic word for "submission," and its converts Muslims, from the Arabic for "one who surrenders." The new faith would have profound social and political as well as religious consequences. It would unite the autonomous, feuding tribes of the Arabian Peninsula into a powerful federation that would sweep through the Middle East and beyond, creating within the span of a single century an empire stretching from India to Spain.

Muhammad—whose name means worthy of praise—was a member of the Quraysh tribe, which had settled the Arabian town of Mecca during the previous century. By the time of Muhammad's birth around the year 570, the Quraysh were among the most powerful of the tribal kinship groups who populated the scattered towns and oases of Arabia or herded their camels, sheep, and goats as desert nomads. These tribes in turn were

While family members look on from the sides, a pair of angels cradles the infant Muhammad and five midwives minister to his mother, Amina. Inspired by Christian paintings of the birth of Christ, such nativity scenes are rare in Islam, which claims nothing miraculous about the Prophet's birth.

subdivided into clans, which were extended families based on male lineage. Muhammad's own clan was the Hashemites.

During his early years, Muhammad's Hashemite clan had proved vital to his upbringing. His father had died before he was born, leaving his mother virtually destitute, with little more to her name than half a dozen camels and a young slave girl. As was the custom, Muhammad's mother sent her infant son to live for a couple of years with a nomad family in the desert, where the hard, simple life was thought to promote health and character. Muhammad returned home when he was five years old, but his mother died soon after, leaving him in the care of his maternal grandfather. Within two years the grandfather also died, and the

orphan was taken in by his uncle Abu Talib, a leading citizen of Mecca and chief of the Hashemites. Abu Talib made certain young Muhammad became a skilled archer and a competent swordsman and wrestler. Most important, though, he taught the boy the rudiments of tending livestock and the delicate arts of buying and selling, skills necessary in a city like Mecca.

Located in the west of the Arabian Peninsula, Mecca lay in a barren valley unsuitable for farming, but it was a thriving center for trade. Muhammad's great-grandfather had been the first to equip the camel caravans that now regularly left Mecca for the great cities in Syria and Iraq laden with leather, livestock, and metals mined in the nearby mountains. Mecca controlled this

trade by building alliances with the surrounding camel-breeding tribes. Cooperation with these warlike nomads, known as the Bedouin, provided both transportation for caravans and protection against the raiders who threatened the trade routes of Arabia.

Muhammad accompanied his uncle on at least one caravan trip to Syria and later began to lead expeditions of his own. The young merchant soon developed a reputation for trustworthiness and was referred to as *al-Amin*—"the Reliable." When he was about 25, his reputation came to the attention of an older woman named Khadija, a rich widow who equipped caravans for the trek to Syria. Impressed by Muhammad's work and character, Khadija hired him as an agent to lead one of her camel trains.

Shortly afterward Khadija proposed marriage, and Muhammad accepted.

The marriage seems to have been a happy one. In a society where polygamy was commonly—though not universally—practiced, Muhammad was devoted to Khadija and took no other wives while married to her. She bore him at least six children— two boys, who died in infancy, and four girls. Muhammad treated them with indulgence and playfulness, joining in their games and letting the youngsters climb on his back and ride him like a horse.

Muhammad and Khadija had been married for about 15 years when he received his first message from God on Mount Hira. These periodic revelations, which verse by verse constituted the growing body of the Koran, often came to Muhammad in the midst of ordinary activities. He would swoon and break into

In this representation of the wedding ceremony of Muhammad and his first wife, Khadija, the painter has crowned the bride *(far right)* and bridegroom with flamelike halos and covered their faces with veils. Muslim artists were wary of painting the faces of the Prophet and his family, lest the portraits be inaccurate or sacrilegious.

The city of Mecca, home of Muhammad and a site of pilgrimage in pre-Islamic and Islamic times, is represented on this colorful tile designed to adorn a pulpit. In the center of the city stands the cube-shaped Kaaba shrine, draped with black brocade.

a sweat, each experience so powerful that it left him feeling his "soul had been torn away." Khadija would then take her shaken husband in her arms and hold him, soothing him until he stopped trembling. But even more alarming than receiving the revelations was not receiving them. After his first few messages around the year 610, he felt that Allah was no longer speaking to him. The heavens, it seemed, had closed, and Muhammad fell into despair.

After two years the revelations resumed, however, and Muhammad's prophetic ministry began quietly in Mecca. Khadija was his first convert. Other early followers included young Ali, whom Muhammad had made a member of his household after his own two sons died in infancy, and a former slave named Zayd. Three years later another revelation from Allah instructed him, "Warn thy family, thy nearest relations," prompting Muhammad to host the dinner party for his clan in 615. Now he was ready to take his message beyond his own Hashemite clan and into the streets of Mecca.

All around the city, the ancient tribal values of honor and generosity were being eroded. Business relationships were replacing the customary ties of kinship, and rich merchants, preoccupied with their pursuit of wealth, were ignoring the traditional practice of taking care of orphans and the disadvantaged. Muhammad was dismayed at the rampant materialism of his city and declared that the wealthy should give a tenth of their income to the poor. Craftsmen, shopkeepers, and those Meccans who had fallen behind economically were attracted to the message, and they began to follow the Prophet, the one "who speaks things from heaven," through the streets.

From many of his fellow Meccans, however, Muhammad encountered nothing but mockery and derision. They accused him of having received his revelations from human rather than divine sources, of letting his imagination run away with him, of practicing sorcery and witchcraft, of being mad. They resented the inconvenient prescription that all Muslim converts must, after ritual washing, prostrate themselves in prayer five times a day. And they bridled when "the Messenger of God," as Muhammad had come to be known, began to preach belief in one universal God and to criticize the traditional pagan gods of Arabia.

Monotheism was not a new concept in Arabia; both Christians and Jews had long lived in the peninsula. But fidelity to the deities of the past had an economic as well as a spiritual incentive. In the middle of Mecca stood the Kaaba, a small boxlike structure that housed a sacred black stone; the shrine was said to be where the pagan god Hubal and 360 other local deities dwelled. Pilgrims from across Arabia would travel to the Kaaba to pay homage to the gods, then stop to sip the blessed waters of the nearby well of Zamzam. The pilgrims needed provisions while in the city and invariably left with their purses a little lighter.

Alarmed by the teachings and growth of Islam, the city fathers launched a campaign of violent harassment of Muhammad and his followers. To avoid trouble, groups of Muslims would travel outside the town to perform their rituals. One day, however, the Muslims were interrupted by a crowd of Meccans, who began to taunt them. A fight broke out and a convert named Saad ibn Abi Waqqas, a cousin and trusted companion of Muhammad, wounded one of the Meccans with the jawbone of a camel. Tradition holds that this was the first blood shed in the name of Islam.

Opposition to the Muslims intensified. When an African slave named Bilal became a convert, his owner punished him by tying him up and leaving him exposed to the sun with a huge stone weighing down his chest. Undaunted, the slave proclaimed the uniqueness of Allah, shouting, "One! One!" His suffering ended when one of Muhammad's friends and fellow believers, a merchant named Abu Bakr, purchased the slave and then set him free.

To avoid persecution, many Muslims fled from

A Bedouin tribeswoman tends a camel herd, her means of survival in the harsh desert environment of Arabia. Camels are loved by the Bedouin, who kiss their favorite animals, call them by name, and even make up poems about them.

The Bedouin: People of the Desert

For thousands of years, nomadic Bedouin have roamed the trackless deserts of Arabia in search of water and pasture. Shunning the lifestyle of the settled communities established along the desert fringes, the Bedouin lead a life of great hardship and deprivation, a way of life made possible through the agency of a remarkable creature: the single-humped camel native to the deserts of the Middle East.

The camel served the Bedouin as both transport and provider of food and materials, as war-horse, and as unit of exchange. A healthy adult camel could travel 60 miles a day across the desert carrying up to 400 pounds. It could go three days without water in summer's blistering heat and even longer in winter. The Bedouin wove tents and ropes from its hair, tanned its skin into leather, burned its dried dung as fuel, drank its milk, and on occasion feasted on its flesh. Large sums, such as the dowry of a bride, were counted in numbers of camels.

A second mainstay of Bedouin life was the date palm, its nourishing fruit obtained through trade with the oasis settlements. In addition to providing the Bedouin with an easily preserved food, the dates could be fermented into wine, their pits crushed into feed for the tribe's camels, and the fronds of the palm tree woven into baskets or used for housing and fences. The date palm, one proverb declared, was "the mother and the aunt of the Arabs."

Despite its nomadic nature, Bedouin society was knit together into a tight fabric of tribal loyalties and alliances. "Be loyal to thy tribe," sang a desert bard. "Its claim upon its members is strong enough to make a husband give up his wife." In return, the tribe would protect its members and succor them in times of need. An insult to one was an insult to all and required vengeance. Yet each member had a proud sense of independence and equality, and whatever their wealth, all tribesmen were subject to the unbreakable ties of custom and lineage.

The hard desert life led inevitably to competition among the tribes for the limited number of wells and grazing areas. In accordance with the desert code, a Bedouin might kill his last camel to feed a stranger; but if he needed another camel, he simply took it. As a result, armed bands were constantly rustling the livestock from rivals' encampments or waylaying stragglers along the caravan routes. The objective was plunder, not combat. Blood called for blood in the tribal ethic, and spilling it could spark a feud that no one wanted.

Even so, tribal feuds were constantly breaking out, providing the raw material for the desert Arabs' most highly developed art form: poetry, the power of the spoken word. The classic Arabic of the desert was an extraordinarily expressive medium. A man endowed with eloquence had great influence with his fellow Arabs, and a man gifted with the very words of God could demand of them almost anything.

Wind-shaped dunes soar up to several hundred feet in the al-Dahna desert of central Arabia. The interior of the peninsula is so dry that it contains not a single perennial stream; temperatures drop below freezing at night in winter and rise above 130 degrees Fahrenheit in summer.

The Holy Book of Islam

According to the teachings of Islam, the Word of God was revealed by five major prophets in the time before Muhammad: Adam, Noah, Abraham, Moses, and Jesus. Accordingly, Jews and Christians were, like Muslims, considered "people of the book." The Muslims believed, however, that over time the Jewish and Christian Scriptures—the Torah and the Bible—were corrupted; humans no longer followed the will of God, and a new revelation was needed. Delivered by the archangel Gabriel to the prophet Muhammad, this message was known as the Koran, Arabic for the "Recital" or the "Reading." It would be the last communication from God to humankind, a guide to lead the faithful until the Day of Judgment.

As God's final Word, the Koran was believed by Muslims to be infallible. During the two decades that Muhammad received the divine messages, his followers either memorized them or wrote them down; the recitation of these revelations then formed a part of Islamic worship. Some of the most devout Muslims—the "guardians" of the revelation—memorized the entire Koran, an amazing feat of piety when it is considered that this holy book, almost as long as the Christian New Testament, con-

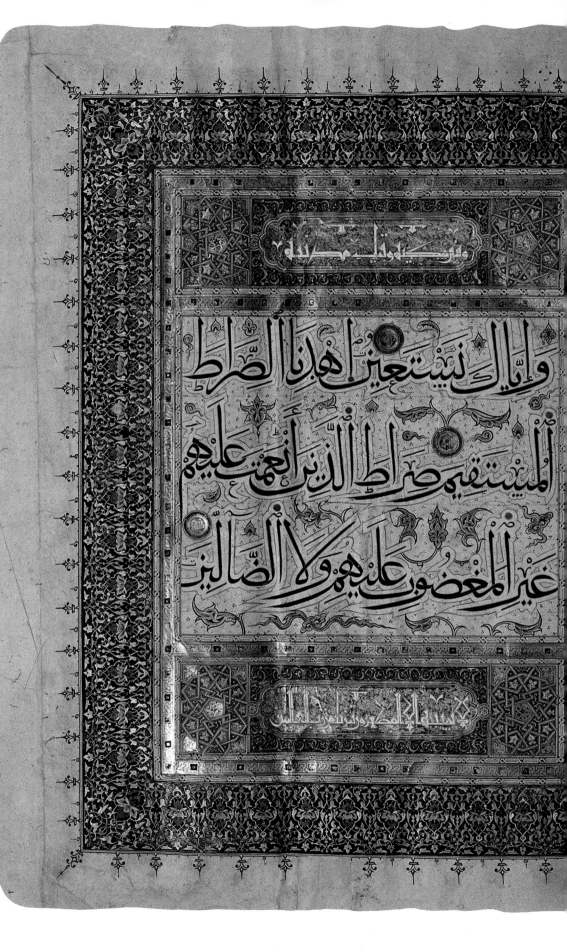

tains 6,000 verses and around 78,000 words.

After the Prophet's death, his closest associates took steps to preserve the revelations. They decided that all existing versions of the Koran should be collected and examined by a committee of Muhammad's Companions, headed by one of his scribes. From these texts, a standardized copy of the holy book was produced; all other versions were destroyed.

Since no one was completely sure of the order in which Muhammad had received his revelations, the Koran's 114 chapters, or suras, were arranged according to length. The longest ones, which were placed first, were the most legalistic and instructive, fundamental to the organization and regulation of Muslim life: "Here is a plain statement to men," declared one of the early chapters, "a guidance and instruction to those who fear God." At the end of the Koran come the short, ecstatic suras revealed in the first eruption of the Prophet's inspiration; they are mainly concerned with warnings about Judgment Day and the hellfire awaiting those who worshiped more than one god.

Geometric designs around Arabic inscriptions create a dazzling effect in the opening pages of this Koran, commissioned by a 14th-century ruler of Egypt for his mother.

The next morning the Meccans approached from the east. Vultures wheeled overhead and perched on rocky slopes in the rear of both armies. The battle began with one-on-one combat between three warriors from each side, as was the Arabian custom. Muhammad then lined up the dismounted Muslims in close formation, promised that any of them who died fighting that day "advancing not retreating" would immediately "enter Paradise," and ordered them to bombard the enemy with arrows. Unlike the Meccans, who fought with bravado but no discipline, the Muslims had been well drilled by their leader. On command, they surged forward, slashing with their swords. In the heat of the hand-to-hand fighting, many of the Muslims were certain that they had help from on high, from a host of angels that rode all around them, mounted on horses whose hoofs never touched the ground.

By noon the Muslims had routed the enemy. The Meccans fled in disarray, leaving some 50 of their men dead and about the same number captive. The victors started to round up prisoners for execution, but Muhammad stopped them: A revelation had told him the captives could better serve the cause if they were spared. He made a few exceptions, though; a Meccan who had composed derogatory verses about Muhammad was put to death, as was a man who claimed that his stories about Persia were as good as the stories of the Koran. Meanwhile, the original target, the caravan, had managed to make it back to Mecca. Even so, the Muslims rode home to great acclaim in Medina. They had been successful in their first jihad—a word that literally meant struggle but came to stand for holy war.

With his authority strengthened by the victory at Badr, Muhammad began to crack down on those he had come to perceive as his enemies in Medina—the Jews. After his emigration, he had regarded Medina's Jews as members of his community. He had even adopted some of their practices, commanding his followers to pray in the direction of Jerusalem, Judaism's ancient shrine, and to observe with fasting the Jewish Day of Atonement. But he was surprised and hurt by the failure of Medina's Jews to accept him as a

MUHAMMAD'S WIVES

Known as "the mothers of the believers," Muhammad's wives were held in high regard within the Islamic community. However, their special status also meant certain restrictions on their behavior and dress, and they were prohibited from remarrying after the Prophet's death.

Of the dozen or so women Muhammad married over the course of his life, his first wife, Khadija, was his favorite. "She believed in me when I was rejected," Muhammad once declared. "When they called me a liar, she proclaimed me truthful. When I was poor, she shared with me her wealth and Allah granted her children though withholding those of other women."

One of those children was their oldest daughter, Fatima, who also seems to have occupied a special place in Muhammad's heart. When Fatima's husband, Ali, sought the Prophet's permission to take another wife, his father-in-law was unsympathetic. Declaring "What hurts her, hurts me," he turned down the young man's request.

In his later years, Muhammad was particularly fond of Aisha, his youngest wife. But Aisha never fully replaced Khadija in his affections. In the picture at left, which shows a servant unwrapping a gift from the archangel Gabriel to Fatima, Muhammad and three members of his family are shown veiled and with halos above their heads. Significantly, it is young Aisha *(center)* who reaches out to hold her husband's hand but Khadija's daughter Fatima who sits in the position of honor next to the Prophet.

prophet and angered by the mocking hostility some of them had demonstrated toward the Muslims. After two years in Medina he changed the time of fasting to Ramadan—the ninth month of the Muslim year—and altered the direction of prayer to Islam's birthplace, Mecca. Increasingly he saw Medina's Jews as a threat to his new kind of religious and political community.

Muhammad's jihad against Mecca became the context for his war against the Jews. After the Battle of Badr he seized upon a trivial dispute in Medina that had resulted in the deaths of a Muslim and a Jew to expel one of the town's Jewish tribes and claim its property. A year later a Meccan army dealt the Muslims a severe defeat on the slopes of Uhud, a hill a few miles from Medina; Muhammad diverted his disheartened disciples by driving out another Jewish tribe, which, he claimed, was plotting his assassination. In 627, after Medina had withstood a two-week siege by 10,000 Meccans, he accused the town's remaining Jews of collaborating with the enemy. This time, though, instead of exiling them, he let an Arab chief from Medina who was their bitter enemy decide their fate. The chief sold all the women and children into slavery; the men—more than 600 in all—he had beheaded.

It was during this time of struggle and warfare that Islamic policy on marriage emerged. The battle at the hill of Uhud had cost the lives of nearly 70 Muslims and left many families fatherless. A new revelation to Muhammad enabled him to deal with the sudden increase in unattached women, unmarried daughters as well as the recently widowed. Men who had only one wife were now encouraged to take as many as four. Having multiple wives was an old practice among Arab men. The new injunction, which actually *limited* believers to four wives, served as a kind of social legislation. The husband had to treat each wife equally in every way and had to promise to administer the property of fatherless young women equitably.

Muhammad himself was allowed as many wives as he liked, however, and during his later years in Medina had nine spouses at once. Some were widows of Muslim warriors to whom he felt an obligation. Others he married in order to cement political alliances. His harem was housed in his residence, a mud-brick building that also served as a mosque, or place of worship. For each new wife a small apartment was built as an addition to the mosque. The courtyard of the mosque was used for the community's five-a-day formal prayers. Before dawn a muezzin, or crier, would climb to the roof of the highest house in the neighborhood. When the sun rose, he would call out in his resonant voice, urging the faithful to prayer.

Around this time, a further revelation came to Muhammad on the subject of Muslim women. Known in the Koran as the Verses of the Curtain, it instructed the Prophet to seclude his wives from the rest of the community. There were practical reasons for such a move. Men congregating in the nearby courtyard of the mosque would frequently approach Muhammad's wives in order to obtain favors from the Prophet, and he could effectively end this practice by restricting access to his wives. Seclusion had another benefit: It prevented any contact between his wives and other men that might be labeled scandalous and thus employed by his enemies to discredit him. Accordingly, he forbade his wives to visit the courtyard when outsiders were there, and within his household he raised a curtain to hide his harem from the sight of any male visitors. This curtain was called the *hijab*. Eventually, the word would come to have an additional meaning—veil—and future generations of Muslim women would be required to cover their faces when they appeared in public.

The crowning episode in Muhammad's remarkable life occurred early in the year 632. By that time he had already won the political or religious allegiance of most of the nomadic tribes of Arabia. His long struggle against Mecca had ended triumphantly two years earlier when he marched on his birthplace with 10,000 men and the city had capitulated with scarcely any bloodshed; en masse the Meccans had embraced Islam. Muhammad had ordered the smashing and burning of the pagan idols that dwelt in the Kaaba shrine in the middle of the city. But for the shrine itself Muhammad had other plans. Believing that it had originally been built by the biblical prophet Abraham and his son Ishmael—regarded respectively as the first monotheist and the ancestor of the Arabs—Muhammad ordained the newly purified Kaaba as the house of God. And now, in February 632, he made preparations to lead a pilgrimage, or hajj, from Medina to the Kaaba shrine.

Pilgrimages to the Kaaba had been conducted by Arabs from

all over the peninsula for hundreds of years—but always to worship the shrine's pagan idols. This would be the first hajj in which the ceremonies would be performed by Muslims alone. Thereafter a hajj would be regarded as one of the five "pillars of Islam"—along with fasting, almsgiving, prayer, and confession of faith—and a duty to be undertaken at least once in a believer's lifetime.

Muhammad made the trip from Medina to Mecca accompanied by some 30,000 of the faithful. Along the way, the pilgrims had to abide by a strict set of rules; violence of any kind was forbidden, as were sexual relations, lascivious talk, and quarreling. When on March 3 the great column came within sight of the city, the Prophet, seated atop a camel, raised his right hand in supplication. "Here I am at your service, O God!" he cried. The words, repeated by the ranks of pilgrims for miles behind him, had special resonance for those emigrants for whom this hajj was actually a homecoming to Mecca.

As he led the pilgrims through the city, Muhammad attempted to root the hajj in the sacred traditions of the Arabs. A key part of the pilgrimage was to walk around the Kaaba seven times and to kiss, embrace, and stroke its sacred black stone. The pilgrims also rushed back and forth seven times between two hillocks near the Kaaba—Safa and Marwa—in remembrance of the time when Abraham's wife Hagar frantically searched in the desert for water for her infant son Ishmael. They threw pebbles at the three pillars representing Satan at Mina, just outside the city. And they slaughtered sheep in commemoration of Abraham's willingness to submit to the will of God.

The climax of the hajj came on the slopes of Mount Arafat. This so-called Mount of Mercy stood a dozen or so miles east of Mecca. There Muhammad preached a sermon and imparted the final words of revelation from God that would complete the Koran. The multitude prayed and meditated until sunset, with the words of the Prophet echoing from the hillside. "O men, listen to my words," he cautioned. "I do not know whether I shall ever meet you in this place again after this year."

True to his intuition, this *was* Muhammad's final visit to Mecca—his fabled "pilgrimage of farewell." Three months later, back in Medina in the apartment of his young wife Aisha, Muhammad was stricken by a sudden illness and died. He

Following his nearly bloodless conquest of Mecca in 630, the Prophet *(center, rear)* and his followers remove pagan idols from the Kaaba shrine. Once cleansed and rededicated, the ancient structure became the spiritual center of Islam.

was about 62 years old. He left nine widows, four daughters, and a stunning political and religious legacy. His prophetic mission was complete. Scarcely more than two decades after he heard the voice of the angel Gabriel on Mount Hira, Muhammad and his new faith had come to dominate the Arabian Peninsula.

Muhammad's legacy was enormous, but what he had *not* left behind was a mechanism to appoint his successor; with the death of its prophet, the Muslim community was thrown into chaos. Few had foreseen the consequences of his death. All major legal and religious decisions had been made alone by Muhammad, who had declared that he was the last messenger of God. Now that Muhammad was gone, Islam was rudderless.

In the ensuing vacuum, several rival groups sought to establish their dominance. The early converts from Mecca formed one party, the native Medinans another. Immediately after his death the groups met to decide how to choose a successor to the Prophet. In the end, a compromise candidate was agreed upon. Muhammad's good friend and father-in-law, Abu Bakr, was selected as the new political and religious leader of Islam. He was also the first man to bear the title *khalifa,* or caliph, "successor of Muhammad."

Abu Bakr's first task was to bring back into the fold several Arab tribes who were now preparing to go their own ways. These tribes maintained that they had pledged their loyalty to a leader, not an ideology, and that with the Prophet's death they were released from further obligation. Abu Bakr knew that such defections at this critical stage would be disastrous for the future of Islam. Quickly the caliph moved against the rebellious tribes-

men and, after a year of bitter, bloody conflict, succeeded in reestablishing Muslim dominance throughout the peninsula. But Abu Bakr knew that the job was not yet done. To maintain the unity of the tribes of Arabia—and to make the most of their warrior traditions—he began to mobilize a great Muslim army. Abu Bakr cast his eyes northward for ways to use it.

Most of the lands to the north of Arabia, from Spain in the west to central Asia in the east, were under the control of two great empires: the Byzantine and the Sassanian. But the two imperial powers had grown weak after decades of battling. Seeing his opportunity, Abu Bakr launched a series of raids against both, sending his tribesmen into the Byzantine province of Syria and into the Sassanian territories in Iraq.

Abu Bakr never lived to see the fruits of what he had started. In 634 he died. On his

"Good news! The Persians have given us the soil of their country."

deathbed, however, he made clear the name of the man he had chosen as his successor, a close associate of Muhammad's: Umar ibn al-Khattab.

As caliph, Umar escalated the raids of his predecessor into full-scale invasions, and Arab warriors swept into Palestine and Syria. When the Byzantines dispatched an army to confront them, the Muslims faded into the desert. In that familiar environment, the Muslims bided their time. The following year, 25,000 Arab horsemen galloped out of the haze of a desert sandstorm to overwhelm a Byzantine force twice that size. Damascus fell to the invaders, followed by the cities of Antioch and Aleppo. In late 637 the Muslims seized the holy city of Jerusalem.

With much of Syria under his control, Caliph Umar declared a holy war against Iraq, heartland of the great Mesopotamian empires of ancient times and the westernmost province in the Sassanian empire of Persia. To lead his troops he called upon the veteran Muslim soldier Saad ibn Abi Waqqas.

Then age 40, Saad had a distinguished pedigree as a warrior in the cause of Islam. One of the leading men in the exclusive class known as Companions—the early converts and associates of Muhammad—he was the man who when younger had shed the first blood in defense of the new faith, striking a Meccan opponent with the jawbone of a camel. He had also fired the first arrow for Islam, it was said, and had taken part in the Battle of Badr and all the other early military engagements. According to tradition, this short, thickset man with a large head and shaggy hair was one of 10 to whom the Prophet had promised entry into paradise. And now the Prophet's successor, Caliph Umar, had chosen him to strike against Iraq.

Saad rose to the challenge. By early 637 he had marched his army to the banks of the Euphrates River in central Iraq. There his men made camp, subsisting on meat from herds of sheep and camels sent on the hoof from Medina and on whatever grain they were able to plunder from the surrounding Iraqi towns. Meanwhile, Saad dispatched a delegation to the Sassanian court.

Twenty warriors were sent across the Euphrates to Ctesiphon, the capital of the 21-year-old Sassanian king, Yazdegerd. The rough clothing, crude weapons, and unkempt appearance of the Arabs drew contemptuous smiles as they were led into the audience hall of Yazdegerd's palace. Yet these men of the desert were unfazed by the splendor they saw around them. Their spokesman even had the gall to invite Yazdegerd to become a Muslim himself, or at least to agree to pay tribute to the Arabs and place himself under their protection. The haughty young king was outraged. In fact, were the visitors not protected by the immunity granted to ambassadors, he would have killed them on the spot. Instead, he called for a sack of earth and had it loaded onto the back of the Arab spokesman before sending him and his companions away. The king intended the gesture to be a sign of his contempt, but the delighted Muslims rode back to their camp and presented the sack of earth to their general, Saad ibn Abi Waqqas. "Good news!" they cried. "The Persians have given us the soil of their country."

The Sassanian king ordered his general Rustam to give battle immediately. Rustam was a cautious man. He knew that as long as his army was undefeated and intact, the Arabs would be unable to cross the Euphrates except in small raiding parties. He also knew that an army that fought with its back to a river, if defeated, would likely be destroyed. But King Yazdegerd was impatient for victory against these desert nomads, and he would wait no longer. Reluctantly, Rustam built a bridge across the river and moved his army to the west bank.

Arab sources would later claim that the Sassanian force that crossed the Euphrates was 60,000 or even 120,000 strong. Whatever its number, it was undoubtedly larger than Saad's army of around 30,000 men. The Arabs had taken up position on the plain of Qadisiya. Like Rustam, Saad recognized the advantages of the terrain. Ahead of him lay the river, to his back the familiar desert, the ground his Arab warriors knew best. He may well have reflected with satisfaction on the counsel of an earlier Arab commander who had fought against the Sassanians. "Fight the enemy in the desert," General Muthanna had advised Saad before dying of battle wounds. "The Persians cannot follow you there and from there you can return again to the attack."

As the Sassanians deployed for battle on the plain before them, the Arab warriors stood in reverent silence. In front of each tribal contingent a comrade recited from the chapter in the Koran that describes Muhammad's stirring victory over the Meccans at the Battle of Badr. "O Prophet, urge on the believers to battle," the passage began. "If there be of you twenty steadfast, they shall conquer two hundred and if there be of you one hundred, they shall conquer a thousand of the unbelievers."

In keeping with martial custom, several soldiers went forward for individual combat with the Sassanians. After that, the real battle began—lancers advancing on horseback, swordsmen and archers on foot—when suddenly from the Sassanian lines lumbered their most formidable weapons: 33 enormous Asian elephants carrying soldiers crowded into howdahs on their backs. The elephant spearhead threw the Arabs into confusion. Desperately, Arab archers shot at the soldiers riding on the elephants while swordsmen slashed at the straps that secured the howdahs to the backs of the great beasts. Still the elephants kept coming, and the Arabs were lucky to hold their ground until darkness brought to an end the Sassanian attack.

That night, as they always did during a battle, the Arab warriors danced and recited poetry recalling the exploits of their forebears, hoping to spark their waning ardor for combat. But some of the men were grumbling, too. The object of their discontent was their general, Saad ibn Abi Waqqas.

Muslim commanders were expected to lead their troops into combat. But that day, as the fighting raged, Saad lay ill in a small fort behind the lines, suffering from what has variously been described as sciatica or as boils. Even Saad's new wife, Salma, turned on him. She was the widow of Muthanna, the general who had preceded Saad in Iraq, and Saad probably had married her to ensure the loyalty of her late husband's followers. But for the moment at least, his choice of wife was working against him. Disgusted that her husband should stay in bed while his men fought, she goaded him: "O for an hour of Muthanna! Alas there is now no Muthanna." Only when Saad struck her across the face did she end her taunts.

The morning of the second day of battle was spent clearing the dead and wounded from the field. Soon after noon the fighting started again, although this time the Sassanians did not use their elephants, several of whom had been injured the previous day. The first of 6,000 Arab reinforcements arrived that afternoon from Syria, dispatched by Caliph Umar. Some of the new arrivals gamely and repeatedly charged the enemy lines, a number of them riding camels disguised in hoods and drapes in hopes of frightening the Sassanian horses. But the action was inconclusive, and again nightfall brought an end to the fighting.

The following day the Sassanian elephants did line up for battle. Saad, still incapacitated, ordered his lancers to dismount from their horses and approach the dreaded beasts on foot. Jabbing with their lances, the Arabs managed to blind one of the elephants in both eyes, and the great animal began to thrash about in agony, stampeding the others and eventually taking the entire herd out of action.

One of the legends that arose from the repulse of the elephants concerned Abu Mihjan. He was a brave warrior whom Saad had imprisoned for breaking the Koran's injunction against alcohol by getting drunk on wine. The story goes that Abu Mihjan was so eager to fight the enemy that he persuaded one of Saad's concubines to release him on the promise he would return to his fetters after the day's fighting. He mounted Saad's mare, rushed the enemy line, and thrust his sword into the trunk of one of the enemy's elephants. Saad saw the whole thing from the rooftop of the house where he was recuperating behind the lines. "The mare is mine," he declared, "but the charge is that of Abu Mihjan!"

After the fighting ended, as he had promised, the hero returned to his fetters. But the legend has a satisfactory ending: Saad said he would punish him no more for drinking wine, and Abu Mihjan vowed, "By Allah, I shall never drink it again."

As the daylight faded on this third day of battle, the combatants once again returned to their camps. But on this night the lull in the fighting was short-lived. The Bedouin—one of the groups of tribesmen composing the Arab army—decided to launch a night attack on the enemy, priding themselves as they did on their ability to move about in the darkness. The "night of

Seated atop his horse, a prince hunts wild boar in this scene adorning a Sassanian gilded-silver plate. Invading Muslim warriors would have faced such fearsome Sassanian cavalrymen on the plain of Qadisiya in Iraq in 637.

fury," as it was called, unnerved the Sassanians. At dawn the next day the fighting continued, and the stamina bred in the Bedouin by a lifetime of roaming the desert began to tell. Eventually, several Arabs broke through the enemy lines and managed to kill General Rustam. When word spread that the general had been slain, Sassanian resistance collapsed.

In panic, the Sassanians fled from the field. Few of them made it back across the Euphrates bridge. Scattering in all directions, some were cut down on the plain by the pursuing Arabs, others took refuge in nearby marshes, while others were drowned trying to swim across the river. That afternoon the women and children who had accompanied Saad's army moved across the battlefield, where an estimated 8,500 Arabs and even more Sassanians had fallen. The women and children carried goatskins of water to slake the thirst of wounded Muslims and clubs to dispatch any disabled or dying enemy soldiers.

The young Sassanian king, Yazdegerd, withdrew his troops to his capital at Ctesiphon on the east bank of the Tigris River. Without haste, Saad pursued him. Reaching a town on the west bank, just across the river from the capital, Saad and his army made camp. The Sassanians had burned all the Tigris bridges and removed any ferryboats in the area, but at length an informer told Saad of a place where the river could be forded. By the time the Arabs crossed, Yazdegerd and his family had fled north into the Zagros Mountains, and the Arabs took possession of the city unopposed.

Saad established his residence in the royal palace and set up a pulpit in its great banquet hall, which became a mosque where the faithful could gather. His ragged troops paused to gawk at the wonders of the Middle East's most sumptuous city. Some mistook camphor for salt, cooked with it, and were astonished by the bitter taste. Others, who had never seen gold before and knew nothing of its value, traded their shares of it for equal volumes of silver.

At Umar's orders, Saad confiscated for the caliph all the estates that had belonged to the Sassanian king and to those who had fled with him. Other lands were left alone. Both Umar and Saad realized the need to maintain existing levels of agricultural production, and they wanted

Jerusalem: City on a Hill

"Of the ten measures of beauty that came down to the world, Jerusalem took nine." So proclaims an ancient Hebrew text about the city that would become central to three great monotheistic religions. For Jews, Jerusalem is the city of David and Solomon. For Christians, it is the place of Christ's crucifixion. And for Muslims, it was the qibla, or direction of prayer, during the early years of Islam.

These competing claims are reflected in Jerusalem's turbulent history. In AD 324, after centuries of pagan Roman rule, it came under the control of Rome's first Christian emperor, Constantine, who built the Church of the Holy Sepulcher there. The Christian Byzantines ruled Jerusalem until the early seventh century, when first the Persians, then the Arabs conquered the city. Apart from a period of occupation by crusaders in the 12th century, Muslims would rule Jerusalem for the next 1,330 years.

Fifty years after the Muslim conquest, Caliph Abd al-Malik began construction of a new sacred building in Jerusalem. Known as the Dome of the Rock, it replaced an earlier mosque on the Temple Mount, where the Temple of Solomon had once stood. But in choosing the site, the caliph was more mindful of Constantine's church than of the old Jewish temple. "Abd al-Malik, seeing the greatness of the martyry of the Holy Sepulcher and its magnificence," recounted a 10th-century Islamic scholar, "was moved lest it should dazzle the minds of the Muslims and hence erected above the rock the dome which we now see there." The caliph built the shrine over the rock where Abraham supposedly went to sacrifice his son and from which Muhammad made a miraculous night journey to heaven. It has dominated the skyline of the Old City of Jerusalem ever since.

Gleaming in the early morning sun, the gilded roof of the Dome of the Rock rises above the eastern wall of the Old City to dominate the skyline of Jerusalem. Inside, the great dome is supported by a combination of marble columns and piers *(inset)* that encircle the holy rock from which Muhammad is said to have visited heaven.

to make sure that their Bedouin warriors—who were singularly inexperienced as agriculturists—did not seize land and set themselves up as landowners or farmers. In return, the conquered people had to pay the Arabs taxes based on the size and productivity of their fields, as well as a poll tax levied on each individual. With these revenues Saad paid his troops.

Other than collecting the necessary taxes, Umar wanted Saad to interfere in the life of Iraq as little as possible. Although the conquerors gave inducements such as lower taxes to those who converted to Islam, they tolerated other religions and did little proselytizing. Indeed, Umar worried less about the threat posed by the conquered Iraqis than about the potential trouble from the Arab victors. Aware of their rebellious tendencies, he knew he had to keep a tight rein on the unruly tribes that made up his army.

To concentrate the soldiers in one place and prevent their dispersion among the local people, Umar ordered Saad to build a new

around this cluster of buildings allowed room for a marketplace and for camels to be tethered. Radiating in every direction from the town center were the residential districts for each tribe, subdivided into streets or lanes for the various clans. Tribal districts eventually had their own mosques for daily worship and assemblies and even had their own cemeteries. Saad enlisted genealogists to make certain the tribal alignments were accurate.

Around 640 Saad transferred his army from the old capital to Kufa, not long after King Yazdegerd and the remnants of his army had been driven from the mountains of northern Iraq. The Arabs brought with them the doors from the houses they had taken over in Ctesiphon and installed them on their new mud-brick homes. Within a few years the estimated military population of Kufa had grown to 40,000, a number swelled by the thousands of wives and children who came with the soldiers or later migrated to the town.

As the governor of Kufa, with responsi-

"Whoever drowns another will himself be drowned; whoever burns another will be burned."

garrison town. For the site the general selected Kufa, some 80 miles to the southwest on the banks of the Euphrates River, not far from the battlefield of Qadisiya. The location was well chosen. Unlike other places Saad considered, this one was relatively free of flies and mosquitoes, and it sat, as one observer said, "amid sweet springs and luxuriant gardens." The rich pastureland in the area would be important for grazing the soldiers' sheep, camels, and horses.

Saad paid close attention to the construction and layout of Kufa. His residence, his headquarters as governor, and the mosque, built from baked bricks and marble columns salvaged from some nearby ruins, stood at the very center of town. An open space

bility for both military and civic affairs, Saad was bound to come in for criticism. When Saad built a reed fence and wooden gate around his headquarters compound to muffle the noise from the adjoining marketplace, for example, the caliph sent an emissary to burn down the gate and fence. Such structures, Umar held, were barriers that prevented the citizenry from approaching their governor. Although one source insisted Saad treated the people as if he were "a kind mother," there were other complaints. He was an unjust judge, said his critics, and failed to properly lead the salat, the ritual of formal prayers said five times a day. Whatever the truth, Umar decided to remove Saad from office and bring him back to Medina.

THE CALL TO PRAYER

Prayer, one of the five pillars of Islam, is considered the most important duty of a practicing Muslim. Since the early days of Islam, Muslims have performed this duty five times daily, beginning shortly after dawn when the faithful are awakened by the exhortation of the muezzin, or crier, "Prayer is better than sleep." The other four prayers take place just after noon, late in the afternoon, immediately after sunset, and following nightfall. Below, a muezzin stands atop the Kaaba in Mecca and calls the community to prayer.

This episode, however, did not prevent Umar from remembering Saad's sterling qualities when the caliph was mortally wounded by a disgruntled Christian slave in 644. As Umar lay dying, he selected Saad as a member of the *shura*, a council of senior Companions of the Prophet who would choose Umar's successor as caliph. Umar even reportedly told the shura that they could name Saad as caliph if they so wished and that, in any case, the man they chose should consult with the general on matters of state.

But the shura named one of their own, a wealthy Meccan named Uthman. Over the next dozen years the new caliph filled many high offices with his own relatives from the Umayyad clan, effectively curtailing the influence of the other Companions. Revolts against Uthman broke out across the provinces. In 656 a large delegation of Arab warriors from Iraq and the recently conquered province of Egypt brought their grievances to Medina. Finding Uthman unresponsive to their complaints, the warriors broke into his palace, where they discovered him reading the Koran. Without hesitation they attacked their caliph, thrusting their swords into him and spilling his blood over the holy book, which lay open in his lap.

Once used, the regicidal sword would be hard to sheathe. With the help of the mutineers, Ali, a prominent member of the last shura, installed himself as caliph. Ali was Muhammad's ward, cousin, and one of the earliest converts; he was also married to Muhammad's daughter Fatima. Three times he'd been passed over as caliph by his fellow Companions. Now he would have his coveted title, but his empire would be plunged into turmoil.

Thus began the *fitna,* "the time of trial," the first Muslim civil war. Shortly after Ali became caliph, he was challenged by a group of Companions allied with Aisha, Muhammad's youngest widow. Ali decisively defeated this challenge in 656 near the southern Iraqi town of Basra in the Battle of the Camel, so named because the fighting swirled around the vivacious figure of Aisha seated on a camel and vigorously urging her men on with cries and gestures. It was the first major battle between

Above, Muslims swear allegiance to Ali, Muhammad's cousin and son-in-law and the fourth caliph of Islam. Tensions between rival parties continued to trouble the Islamic community, however, finally splitting it into rival Shiite and Sunni factions.

Muslim and Muslim, and like the killing of Uthman it set a dangerous precedent.

The following year Ali had to face a more serious challenge, this time from Damascus, whose governor, Muawiya, was a cousin of the slain Uthman. Muawiya had good reason to challenge Ali: Not only was he seeking vengeance for his kinsman's death, but he also had his eyes on the caliphate itself. In 657 they fought a major battle, which proved inconclusive. But Ali's days as the leader of Islam were numbered. In 661 a disaffected former follower thrust his poisoned dagger into Ali in the mosque of Kufa. Muawiya could now claim the caliphate, if not the satisfaction of personal vengeance.

The old soldier Saad ibn Abi Waqqas, who had shed blood for the Prophet so many years before and who had served Islam with such distinction in Iraq, maintained strict neutrality during all these struggles. He had never put forward any claims to the caliphate himself, though his status would have justified seeking it. Instead, he sat out the civil war at his home near Medina; a decade or so later, unlike the last three caliphs, he died a peaceful and natural death.

After the civil war, Muawiya secured enough support to maintain his position as caliph. But the conflict had left lasting scars on the Muslim community, which was racked by periodic disputes over the rights of succession. Those who accepted the legitimacy of Muawiya became known as the Sunnis. Supporters of Ali were called the Shia, or the Faction; Shiites believed that Ali's two sons were the legitimate heirs because they were the offspring of Muhammad's daughter Fatima and thus direct descendants of the Prophet. A third sect, the Kharijites, or Secessionists, broke off from the Shiites and asserted that the caliph should be elected by the entire Muslim community; his only qualifications, they insisted, should be his piety and moral excellence. Some Kharijites went so far as to consider other Muslims to be infidels worthy only of death, and a Kharijite had been the assassin of Ali.

By ancestry Muawiya was well equipped to deal with these problems. His father,

Enclosed in a litter on her camel, Muhammad's widow Aisha encourages her men at the Battle of the Camel in 656. After her forces were defeated by Caliph Ali, Aisha was taken back to the Iraqi garrison town of Basra, where she lived out the rest of her life.

Abu Sufyan, had led the opposition to Muhammad in Mecca. Muawiya, in fact, was sometimes called "son of the liver eater" because in 625, after a battle between Muslims and Meccans, his mother supposedly had mutilated the corpse of one of Muhammad's uncles and chewed on his liver as an act of vengeance. Later Muawiya's sister married Muhammad, his father converted to Islam, and Muawiya himself—described as one of 17 literate Meccans of the day—served as the Prophet's secretary. (Whether the liver-eating mother was ever reconciled to Islam is not known.)

In 639, after successfully serving in various administrative posts, Muawiya was appointed governor of Syria. He showed himself to be an innovative military leader, commanding an Arab naval force of 200 vessels that defeated a Byzantine fleet in the eastern Mediterranean. He was also a shrewd politician. He made sure that his soldiers lived among the native populations in Damascus and other cities, unlike the Arabs segregated in garrison towns in Iraq and Egypt. To strengthen his position as governor, he did all he could to establish close local ties. Muawiya's most important connection was with the Kalb, a Syrian tribe previously employed by the Byzantines to defend the region against the Sassanians. He sealed this link by marrying the Kalb chief's daughter. Mindful that most Syrians were Christians, he also took as an adviser a member of a Greek Orthodox family who had served the Byzantines in Damascus. Though it caused resentment in Medina, it was no surprise when Muawiya decided to move the capital of the Arab empire out of Arabia and establish it in cosmopolitan Damascus.

Muawiya faced other potential sources of conflict as well, especially from the province of Iraq. There the victorious Arab tribesmen were showing dangerous signs of restlessness. Muawiya well understood their difficulties; these men were raiders and warriors, self-reliant nomads unaccustomed to following the directives of any kind of centralized government. They had to be kept occupied. Muawiya decided to expand the empire through jihad—holy war. Islam was on the march again.

The Arab warriors were spectacularly successful. In 667 they began a series of annual raids on the cities of Bukhara and Samarkand in the east, and in 671 Muawiya transferred some 50,000 tribesmen and their families from the crowded garrison cities of Iraq to the newly conquered eastern province of Khurasan. In the west his troops pushed across North Africa and established the garrison town of Kairouan in modern-day Tunisia. To the north the Arabs occupied the Mediterranean islands of Rhodes and Crete and even laid siege to the Byzantine capital of Constantinople.

Muawiya pacified his growing empire with the old Arab concept of diplomacy known as *hilm*—a combination of cunning patience and skillful manipulation. Whenever possible, he relied on persuasiveness rather than force, dealing with people in such a way that they cooperated without feeling that their dignity had been offended. He employed forbearance, tact, and bribery. He invited Arab tribal leaders to come to court to be flattered and apprised of the merits of his new plan. Then he sent them back to the provinces with suitable presents. When his advisers questioned him about how much he spent on gifts, he replied, "War costs more!" He spelled out his principles of governance this way: "I never use my voice if I can use my money, never my whip if I can use my voice, never my sword if I can use my whip." Then he added, perhaps recalling the blood already spilled in the civil war, "But, if I have to use my sword, I will."

In the conquered provinces beyond Syria, Muawiya ruled through handpicked governors, many of them family members or individuals from his own Umayyad clan. He granted them a great deal of autonomy: The governor organized the army, conducted expeditions aimed at conquering new lands, supervised taxation, preserved order, and led public prayer. He even minted gold and silver coins, which in Iraq, interestingly, bore the portrait of one of the old Sassanian kings, along with the name Muawiya and the legend Commander of the Faithful, the institutional title of the caliphate. The Arab governors typically retained indigenous scribes and other officials from the previous bureaucracies in order to keep troublesome tribesmen away from fiscal affairs and delicate matters of state.

As the Muslim empire expanded, Arab craftsmen adopted many of the artistic techniques of their conquests. This mosaic of village houses from the Great Mosque of Damascus shows the influence of the city's previous, Byzantine rulers, who were accomplished in the art of mosaics. The Great Mosque occupies the former site of a Byzantine church.

Muawiya's most powerful governor was a man named Ziyad, installed in the Iraqi garrison town of Basra. Born to a prostitute in Taif, near Mecca, Ziyad never knew his father. At an early age he'd settled in Basra, where Caliph Ali had defeated the challenge of Muhammad's widow Aisha. Ziyad had supported Ali in his claims to the caliphate, and the latter appointed him governor of a province in southwest Persia. When Muawiya became caliph, he persuaded Ziyad to come over to his side. In fact, Muawiya was so determined to gain Ziyad's loyalty that he publicly claimed him as his half brother, declaring that his own father, Abu Sufyan, also had fathered Ziyad. Ziyad was thus made a member of the ruling Umayyad clan.

Muawiya knew that Iraq still needed a strong hand, and he sent his new half brother there, appointing him governor of Basra around 665. Upon his arrival in the garrison town, Ziyad delivered a stirring inaugural speech in the mosque. He made clear his intention to impose order and to put an end to the custom of personal and familial retaliation: "We have brought a punishment to fit every crime," he told the assembled towns-people. "Whoever drowns another will himself be drowned; whoever burns another will be burned; whoever breaks into a house, I will break into his heart; and whoever breaks open a grave, I will bury him alive in it."

Ziyad let it be known that he would hold tribal leaders responsible for the good conduct of their people and created a force of 4,000 infantry and cavalry to patrol the streets. He also imposed an all-night curfew and made violation of it a capital offense. One of the early violators was a Bedouin who brought his camel into the city in order to sell her milk the following morning. He was arrested and brought before Ziyad. The governor accepted the man's story that he was ignorant of the curfew. But in order to set an example for the rest of the citizens, the law had to be enforced. Ziyad had the man beheaded.

Though brutal, Ziyad's methods apparently had the desired effect. According to one account, on the morning after the first night of curfew, no fewer than 700 heads were found at the gate of Basra's citadel. After the second night, there were 50 heads, and after the third night, only one head—and none thereafter. Ziyad had made his point with relentless severity. He was impartial, if inflexible, and he commanded respect because of it.

Ziyad borrowed freely from the methods of previous Sassanian rulers in formalizing bureaucratic procedures. For example, he instituted a registry department where official documents were sealed with wax and then impressed with his own stamp. The stamp bore the figure of a peacock. He also persuaded the caliph to create his own central registry department after an emissary from Damascus had committed forgery on an unsealed document. Thereafter, any document signed by the caliph was taken to the registry department to be copied. The original document was then tied in a roll, sealed with wax, and stamped with a special mark to maintain secrecy.

Such formalization of government led critics to accuse Muawiya of transforming the caliphate into a traditional monarchy—and with some justification. Like the rulers of the old empires, Muawiya and his governors grew remote from the people. In response to assassination attempts, he created a royal bodyguard of soldiers who escorted him everywhere and had a protective chamber installed in the Great Mosque of Damascus. He established the office of *hajib,* or doorkeeper, to regulate the flow of visitors to his presence. Admission to see Muawiya was typically based on status—or on a good word from friends or relatives favored by the caliph. One doorkeeper was so conscientious that the supplicant he prevented from entering finally got frustrated and broke the doorkeeper's nose. Another visitor was said to have waited at the caliph's gate, huddled in his woolen cloak, for an entire year before he was granted permission to enter.

Suspicions that Muawiya was trying to change the caliphate were confirmed toward the end of his life when he announced his position on the thorny issue of succession. After his death, he declared, his son Yazid should succeed him. No definite rules yet governed the succession, but the caliph always had been formally or informally elected by an inner circle. Now Muawiya was advocating a concept alien to the Arabs—a hereditary dynasty, in this case of the caliph's own Umayyad clan.

Hereditary succession had obvious attractions for an imperial power, which the Arabian state had now become. Upon the death of one caliph, the title would automatically be transferred to his son, thereby avoiding the disruption and uncertainty associated with election. But obtaining a consensus of the tribal leaders on this issue would be no easy matter and required of Muawiya all his diplomatic skills, all his fabled hilm.

As the caliph had pointed out, though, when diplomacy and cajoling failed, threats were always an option. One story tells of a gathering called by Muawiya to promote the principle of hereditary succession. When some of those present expressed disapproval, a tribesman rose to his feet and drew his sword. "The Commander of the Faithful is that one!" he cried, pointing to Muawiya. "And if he dies, then that one!" he announced, indicating the caliph's son Yazid. "And if anyone objects, then this one!" he continued, holding up his sword. The caliph took all this in and then declared, "You are the prince of orators."

Muawiya could rest easy. He had presided over the longest period of peace and prosperity in the short history of the caliphate, and he had gotten his way on succession. By the time he died in 680 at about the age of 80, he had won from his council of elders recognition of Yazid as the next caliph. He was buried beside one of the gates of Damascus. And with his body were interred the little relics he had carried with him since those long-ago days in Medina when he was secretary to Muhammad—fingernail clippings and a few strands of hair from the head of the Prophet.

The Realm of Islam

"Great God, if my advance were not stopped by this sea, I would still go on, to the unknown kingdoms of the West, preaching the unity of thy holy name and putting to the sword the unbelieving nations who worship other gods than thee." So proclaimed Muslim commander Uqba ibn Nafi as he rode along the coast of Morocco in 681. But while the Atlantic may have halted the conquests Uqba undertook in the name of Allah, the spread of the Muslim faith had only just begun.

The march of Islam began in 633, the year following the prophet Muhammad's death, when Arab warriors left their hot, dry, and impoverished homeland in search of fertile fields, water, and wealth—and souls to convert to their new faith. In less than two decades, they had broken the Byzantine and Sassanian empires and conquered Palestine, Syria, Egypt, Iraq, and much of Persia. But it was the second great wave of expansion, under the Umayyad dynasty, that more than doubled their empire by carrying the jihad simultaneously into western Europe, North Africa, and central Asia. By 750 the area dominated by Islam stretched from the shores of the Atlantic Ocean to the Indus River valley in modern-day Pakistan.

Over the next seven centuries, Islam expanded to include areas of sub-Saharan Africa, Africa's east coast, and parts of China and India. Eventually the faith claimed the Malay Peninsula and the islands of Indonesia as well.

Force was often used, but some regions voluntarily accepted their new Arab rulers and found their authority relatively benign. The Arabs usually left administrative duties to local leaders, respected existing titles to land, and tolerated other religions. But whether by military or peaceful means, the mission was clear—to unite the subjugated lands under Arab rule and to spread the faith of Allah.

Arab warriors bearing the banner of the prophet Muhammad travel west, spreading their faith, in this illumination from a Spanish manuscript.

North Africa

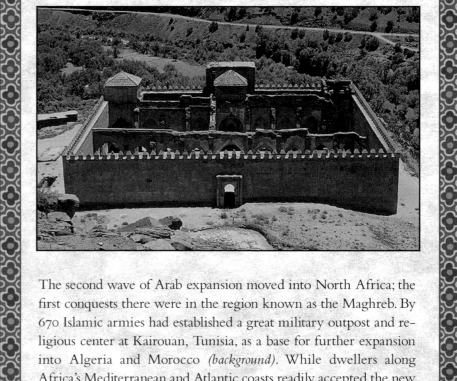

The second wave of Arab expansion moved into North Africa; the first conquests there were in the region known as the Maghreb. By 670 Islamic armies had established a great military outpost and religious center at Kairouan, Tunisia, as a base for further expansion into Algeria and Morocco *(background)*. While dwellers along Africa's Mediterranean and Atlantic coasts readily accepted the new faith, the nomadic Berber tribes of the interior resisted conversion. However, by the 12th century, they too had embraced Islam, and in 1153 they built the fortified Friday Mosque of Tinmal *(above)*.

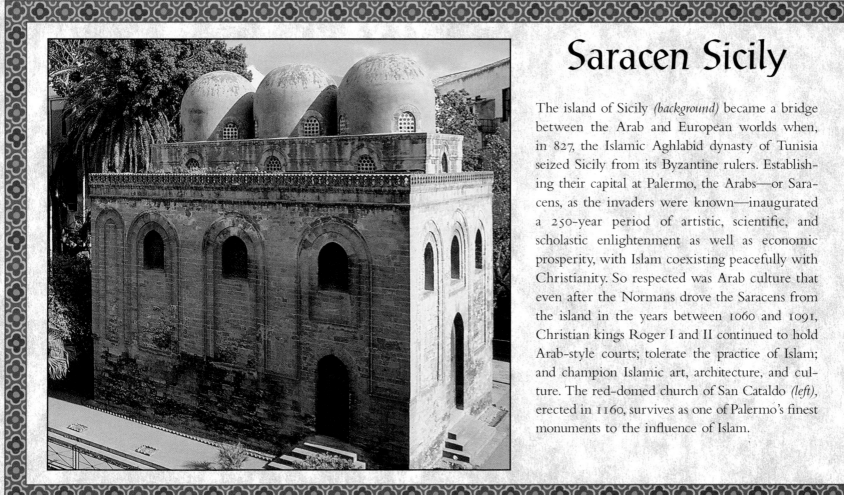

Saracen Sicily

The island of Sicily *(background)* became a bridge between the Arab and European worlds when, in 827, the Islamic Aghlabid dynasty of Tunisia seized Sicily from its Byzantine rulers. Establishing their capital at Palermo, the Arabs—or Saracens, as the invaders were known—inaugurated a 250-year period of artistic, scientific, and scholastic enlightenment as well as economic prosperity, with Islam coexisting peacefully with Christianity. So respected was Arab culture that even after the Normans drove the Saracens from the island in the years between 1060 and 1091, Christian kings Roger I and II continued to hold Arab-style courts; tolerate the practice of Islam; and champion Islamic art, architecture, and culture. The red-domed church of San Cataldo *(left)*, erected in 1160, survives as one of Palermo's finest monuments to the influence of Islam.

West Africa

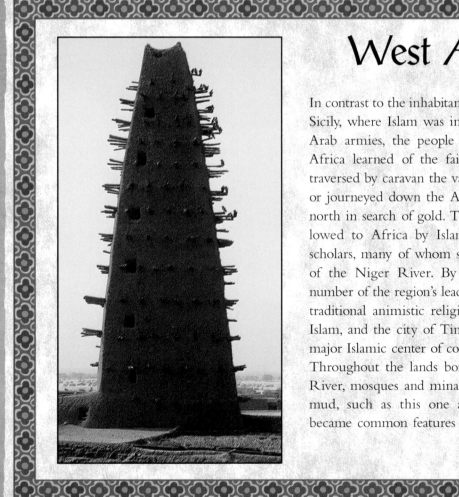

In contrast to the inhabitants of the Maghreb and Sicily, where Islam was introduced by invading Arab armies, the people of sub-Saharan West Africa learned of the faith from traders who traversed by caravan the vast Sahara *(background)* or journeyed down the Atlantic coast from the north in search of gold. These traders were followed to Africa by Islamic proselytizers and scholars, many of whom settled along the bend of the Niger River. By the 11th century, a number of the region's leaders had replaced their traditional animistic religions with the faith of Islam, and the city of Timbuktu had become a major Islamic center of commerce and learning. Throughout the lands bordering on the Niger River, mosques and minarets built of sunbaked mud, such as this one at Agadez in Niger, became common features in the arid landscape.

Islamic India

As early as 713, Arab armies had carried their faith east from Persia and Afghanistan into the Indus River valley. But not until the 11th century did they invade central India *(background)*, eventually conquering most of the subcontinent and establishing sultanates in Delhi and outlying provinces. To commemorate the victory in Delhi, new ruler Qutb ad-Din Aybak erected the Qutb minaret *(above)* and its adjacent mosque on the site of Delhi's Hindu and Jain temples in 1192. With its inscriptions in both Arabic and Sanskrit, the minaret stands as India's oldest Islamic monument.

Central Asia

Sometimes called the "roof of the world," central Asia's Pamir Mountains *(background)* have long been a crossroads of commerce, culture, and religion. In this extremely high-altitude region, where the ancient Silk Road led out of China to the West, incursions by the Arabs began as early as the eighth century, taking advantage of the lack of unity among the native Turkic tribes. In the 10th century, the ruler of Kashgar, a city located in the northern part of the region, converted to Islam, and within a century the formerly Buddhist population had followed his lead. Although the region was conquered by the Mongols in the early 13th century and is now part of China, its people remained Muslim. Kashgar's yellow-tiled Aidkah Mosque *(left)*, built in 1442, is the largest Islamic place of worship in China.

CHAPTER TWO

THE REIGN OF THE CALIPHS

A noble lady and her handmaidens listen to a musician playing the *ud*, the Arab forerunner of Europe's lute. The garden setting, the women's richly colored garments, and their mistress's golden headdress all evoke the luxury and pleasantness of life in the royal courts of the medieval Islamic world.

 Cloaked in the sacred mantle of the Prophet, the caliph Harun al-Rashid emerged from the Kaaba, Islam's most venerated shrine, and looked out over the massed ranks of his followers. He saw before him the ruling elite of his empire, the heads of the most important families and the most senior officers of the state, all dressed in flowing garments of the deepest black—the official livery of those who served his dynasty.

A pilgrimage to Mecca was an act of piety required of every male believer at least once in his lifetime. So Harun, escorted by his army and his court, had set out from Raqqa on the Euphrates River and traveled 1,000 miles south along an ancient trade route to reach the holy city. It had been a strenuous journey, even though the caliph had crossed the Arabian Desert in the most luxurious of litters and camped at night in tented pavilions furnished with every comfort he might desire.

Going to Mecca was for Harun a political as well as spiritual journey. At the time of the pilgrimage, in the year 802, the caliph was probably around 40 years old. Yet he had already begun to suffer intimations of mortality. He felt that the moment had come to secure the future of his dynasty.

Harun al-Rashid's ancestral house, the Abbasids, claimed direct descent from one of the Prophet's uncles, al-Abbas. In the middle of the previous century, the Abbasids had stormed out of their strongholds in eastern Persia and wrested control of the Islamic empire from the Umayyads, the dynasty that had ruled since 661. The Abbasids' new dominions extended from the Indus River to the fringes of Algeria, more than 4,000 miles to the west, and from the foothills of the snowcapped Caucasus to the Arabian city of Sanaa, 2,000 miles south.

The Abbasids redrew the political map of the Islamic world, abandoning the old Umayyad capital of Damascus in Syria and building a new imperial city at Baghdad in Iraq. Although of Arab stock, they had absorbed many cultural influences from their Persian neighbors. They introduced a new inclusiveness into the government of the Islamic state, inviting non-Arab converts, Jews, Christians, Zoroastrians, and Buddhists to participate in the large and complex bureaucracy that ran the empire.

Harun al-Rashid, fifth caliph of the dynasty, had come to the Kaaba, the most sacred edifice in Islam's holiest city, to declare his plans for the continuation of his line. The Abbasids did not adhere to the custom of primogeniture; no one assumed that the caliph's eldest son would automatically inherit the throne. Harun was free to name his successor himself.

On either side of the caliph stood his two 16-year-old sons, Amin and Mamun. It was, announced Harun, his express wish that Amin should become caliph after him, with Amin's half brother, Mamun, second in the line of succession.

Just before making this announcement, Harun had held private interviews with both of his heirs in turn, setting out his desired terms and making each one of them sign an individual declaration of assent. These two documents—henceforth known as the Protocols of Mecca—were

now brought forward and read aloud to a congregation of the most powerful men in the Abbasid state. The documents were then carefully rolled up and enshrined within the Kaaba. None of the participants could have failed to notice the significance of this gesture: Harun had elevated his political will into an article of religious faith.

Although bequeathing the caliphate to Amin, Harun did not intend to let Mamun stand idle. He appointed him governor of Khurasan, on the empire's northeastern margin, giving him virtual autonomy over a land that lay many arduous weeks' journey from the capital. The region had been the cradle of Abbasid power, but it remained a place apart—a remote expanse of mountains, deserts, fiercely independent tribal chieftains, and cities where Persian influence was still strong.

Early in the spring of 809, during a military expedition to suppress an uprising in Samarkand, Harun al-Rashid fell ill and died. The new young caliph in Baghdad and his half brother, who was out in the east with their late father's army, began to treat each other warily: There had never been much love lost between them.

They were the sons of two very different mothers. Amin was the offspring of Zubayda, an Abbasid princess in her own right and Harun al-Rashid's official queen; Mamun's mother was a Persian concubine—possibly the daughter of a defeated Khurasani rebel—who did not survive his birth. Although they had spent their early days together in the harem, learning the rudiments of Arabic grammar and poetry from their father's old boyhood tutor, Harun had soon seen fit to separate them, putting their education into the hands of two different teachers. As they grew to manhood, the half brothers had attracted the support of rival factions within the court. After the death of their father, tensions escalated between the new caliph in Baghdad and his half brother, ruling over distant Khurasan.

Claims and counterclaims—over Mamun's autonomy in the eastern provinces, over the deployment of troops and the dispo-

Buildings of sunbaked brick rise from the east bank of the Tigris River in this depiction of the great city of Baghdad. Capital of the Muslim empire during the Abbasid dynasty, Baghdad was also a great commercial center— in the words of its eighth-century founder, Caliph al-Mansur, a "marketplace for the world."

sition of confiscated treasure, over Mamun's creation of a new coinage featuring himself and without mention of the caliph—flew back and forth across the 1,000 miles separating Baghdad from Mamun's base in the city of Merv. Less than 18 months after their father's death, the brothers had declared war.

Amin enjoyed the support of the Baghdad aristocracy; Mamun's backers, most of whom hailed from the eastern Persian provinces, represented a diverse collection of communities and interest groups with longstanding grievances against the caliphate. The two sides first met in battle in May 811, around the city of Rayy, on the site of present-day Teheran; the caliph's troops got the worst of it there, and again at Hamadan, before retreating to Baghdad.

As it happened, Mamun's own two sons were still in residence in the capital at this time. When Amin's army commander, a tough tribal leader named Asad, suggested that the boys be taken hostage and used as political pawns, the caliph berated him for even contemplating such an outrage upon his nephews, whom, in accordance with Abbasid custom, he referred to as his own children. "You are a mad Bedouin!" roared Amin. "You call upon me to kill my children and spill the blood of my family! Truly, this is folly and insanity!"

Asad's opposite number, the commander of Mamun's army, was a man named Tahir ibn al-Husayn. Tahir was a scion of an old Arab landowning family that had settled in the town of Bushang, about 500 miles south of Merv, during the days of the Umayyad dynasty but had long since gone native and adopted Persian ways. Spurred on by Tahir, the rebels reached Baghdad in August 812.

For an entire year the capital struggled to survive in a state of siege. When the city's defenses finally crumbled, Tahir hunted down the caliph. On the morning of September 26, 813, the severed head of Amin appeared on one of the city gates, sending shock waves throughout the Islamic world. The Abbasids had carefully fostered the belief

This painting of elegantly attired serving girls once graced the harem wall of a ninth-century Abbasid palace northwest of Baghdad. As they dance, the women pour wine out of round-bodied, long-necked vessels shaped like the early Islamic glass bottle at right. Despite Islam's prohibition of alcohol, drinking parties were still a favorite activity at many royal courts.

that a caliph ruled under Allah's protection and was thus invincible: Tahir, acting in Mamun's name, smashed that illusion with a single stroke.

Instead of ending the civil war, Amin's death brought the state to the brink of chaos, engendering another six years of uprisings, secession attempts, and factional infighting across the provinces. Mamun, still based in Khurasan, was—by the terms of the Mecca protocols—now the caliph, but there remained pockets of dissent, especially in Baghdad itself. In July 817 the inhabitants of the capital swore allegiance to another member of the Abbasid family, Mamun's uncle Ibrahim ibn al-Mahdi, acclaiming him their caliph instead of Mamun.

By 819 the war was over. Ibrahim ibn al-Mahdi scuttled into hiding as Mamun himself finally arrived from the east. On the morning of August 10, the people of the capital lined the streets to watch their rightful caliph make his triumphal entry into Baghdad. What they saw gave them cause for alarm. Mamun, flanked by his entourage of Khurasani warlords, looked nothing like any Abbasid caliph they had ever seen. Instead of the dynasty's traditional black, the caliph and his men wore green. Their short coats, their turbans, even the flags and banners fluttering from their spears and lances were all in the official color of the old Sassanian empire, whose Zoroastrian rulers had governed Persia before the coming of the Umayyads.

By sheer coincidence, shrewd timing, or the will of heaven, the caliph's entry into Baghdad coincided with a near total eclipse of the sun. No one in the crowd could doubt that this portent presaged the birth of a new era. To the Arab families of Baghdad, who saw themselves as the hereditary guardians of Abbasid culture and Islamic orthodoxy, the future looked as dark as that day's skies. Their new caliph, half Persian by birth, had spent many years in a land where the old Zoroastrian traditions were still alive. His inner circle included recent converts to Islam, perhaps even nonbelievers. Would the faith and the state be safe in his hands? Tahir, aware of these undercurrents, quickly persuaded Mamun to abandon the alien green in favor of the familiar, reassuring Abbasid black.

Battered though it was by the long siege, Baghdad still dazzled the provincial warlords in Mamun's entourage. Housing some half a million people and sprawling over 25 square miles on both banks of the Tigris River, it was the largest metropolis in the Middle East, surpassing even the great city of Constantinople. Visitors marveled at its mosques and ornate palaces, its fragrant gardens filled with birdsong, its marketplaces

Science of the Stars

"Look for knowledge," the prophet Muhammad urged his followers, "even as far as China." With fervor and commitment, Arab mathematicians, cartographers, engineers, physicians, and chemists heeded him, and for more than six centuries Arabic was the world's language of science.

Of particular significance were Arab advances in the field of astronomy. Here, as in other disciplines, Muslim scholars inherited much from older cultures, especially those of Persia, India, and Greece. But in astronomy they took existing knowledge and pushed it to new horizons. They discovered new stars, improved the existing Greek astronomical system, and calculated the thickness of the earth's atmosphere. Convinced that the earth was a sphere, Muslim astronomers calculated the length of the meridian that circled the earth near the town of Mosul, and some even postulated that the earth rotated on an axis.

Islamic achievements in astronomy owed much to the astrolabe, a device used to compute the movement of the planets and the position of stars. A Greek invention, the astrolabe was essentially a flat metal disk ranging in size from two inches in diameter

to a foot or more across. The circumference of the astrolabe was marked in degrees, and swinging on a pivot from the center was a pointer called an alidade. The astronomer would suspend the astrolabe by a ring at the top and aim the pointer at a star or some other distant object. The pointer would form an angle with a horizontal line on the astrolabe, and by measuring the number of degrees in the angle, the astronomer could determine the altitude of the star.

With the help of an astrolabe *(above, top)*, a group of astronomers watch the heavens from an observatory at Maragheh in northwestern Persia. For Muslims, the study of astronomy had a divine seal of approval. "It is He," the Koran says of Allah, "Who has appointed for you the stars that by them you might be guided in the shadows of land and sea."

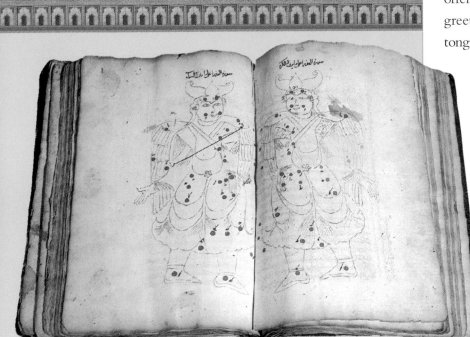

Following ancient Greek tradition, the 10th-century book *El Kitab As Suwar (The Book of Fixed Stars)* represents the heavenly constellations as human or animal figures. Depicted above is the constellation of Gemini, or "the Twins."

Known as "the mathematical jewel," the astrolabe is a computational instrument that was used to measure the height of celestial bodies. As the hand-held copper model at right shows, astrolabes could also be outstanding works of art.

offering the best of everything. The city's streets resounded with greetings, quarrels, gossip, and sales talk in a multitude of Asian tongues. Its inhabitants, whether natives or newcomers, prided themselves on their city's international atmosphere.

As soon as he had settled into his palace, Mamun ordered his secretaries to compile a list of the most intelligent and convivial men in the capital—scholars, courtiers, philosophers, senior army officers of the more reflective sort. These, he declared, were the people he wanted to cultivate as his friends and dinner companions.

Throughout his reign, the caliph sought out wise and witty guests to enliven his leisure hours. But the court was surprised when, in 825, Mamun introduced a new member into his intimate circle: his disgraced uncle, Ibrahim ibn al-Mahdi, the man who had been made caliph by Mamun's opponents during the civil war.

Several years after Ibrahim's flight from the city, Mamun's soldiers had finally tracked him down. The fugitive had been escorted back to Baghdad in fear and trembling. He was brought into Mamun's presence and forced to listen while the caliph and his advisers discussed the various punishments that might be appropriate for his crimes. Execution, said the pundits in attendance, was really the only proper fate for a usurper. The assembled courtiers fell silent. Ibrahim sweated as Mamun pondered.

Finally, looking grave, the caliph announced that he would pardon the traitor. He quoted the Koran: "There is no reproach upon you today. God will forgive you, and He is the most merciful of those showing mercy." Uncle and nephew were reunited, and the court praised their caliph's magnanimity.

Mamun may have been planning to reprieve his uncle all along. Everyone considered Ibrahim a good-natured soul with a quirky sense of humor. Some defenders even suggested that his temporary acceptance of the caliphate may have been nothing more than a joke that misfired. Whatever the truth, Mamun chose to let bygones be bygones. He knew that Ibrahim —famed as a gourmet, a raconteur, and a talented singer—would add spice to evenings at the palace.

Exhilarated by this new lease on life and the prospect of an appreciative audience, Ibrahim went off to polish his musical repertoire. His favorite rehearsal space was the privy sited at the bottom of his garden; an admirer once concealed himself nearby for the pleasure of hearing Ibrahim's voice.

For the epicurean Ibrahim, a royal dinner party was one of life's great joys. All the choicest delicacies of the Islamic world found their way to the caliph's gold- and silver-topped dining tables: apples and apricots from Syria, the pure white honey of Isfahan, sweetened rose-water preserves from the Persian province of Fars, and melons from beyond the Caspian Sea, kept fresh inside leaden boxes packed with snow.

The palace had two kitchens—a small one for the caliph and his chosen companions and a larger one to feed the multitude of courtiers, administrators, artisans, attendants, and entertainers. Together they consumed 50,000 pounds of sugar a year, along with 100,000 pomegranates, 20,000 pounds of raisins, 15,000 pounds of mango jam, and 1,000 pounds of dried peaches from the orchards at Rayy.

Ibrahim's enthusiasm for fine food had inspired him to write a cookbook, the first of its kind produced in Arabic. He took pride in creating elaborate recipes, setting some of them down in verse. One of his inventions, so costly it left even the caliph gasping, was a dish consisting of hundreds of tiny fish tongues, all exquisitely sculpted and reassembled to form a single, giant sea creature, complete with eyes, mouth, tail, and gleaming scales.

Food, however fascinating, was not the only object of attention at the caliph's table. The quality of the conversation was as important as the quality of the cuisine. Mamun and his companions, dressed for the occasion in immaculate red linen or gold-embroidered brocade, regaled one another with witty stories, nostalgic reminiscences of days and friends long departed, and free-flowing philosophical discussions.

After the meal, Mamun might summon the talented slave woman named Arib to join him for a round of chess, which, as he liked to tell any onlookers, "sharpens the intellect." He enjoyed staging chess tournaments, inviting well-known adepts to pit their wits against each other in his presence or challenging them to join him in a game. But he was frustrated by the formal etiquette of the game, by players who made their moves in somber silence. "Chess and politeness," he scolded, "do not go well together! Talk naturally as you would among yourselves."

Three royal falconers hasten after their quarry in this lively 12th-century ivory carving of a hunt scene. Hunting was a favorite pastime of the Abbasids, who trained a wide range of animals, including hounds, weasels, ferrets, and—most prized of all—cheetahs, to assist in the chase.

Another favorite, less sedentary, pastime was hunting. Mamun loved the chase. Mounted on the finest and fastest horses, he and his companions pounded off in pursuit of game birds, deer, wild boar, and even lions. Not all their quarry was destined to be skinned or eaten, however; since the early days of the dynasty, the Abbasid caliphs had enthusiastically collected examples of every species of living creature that could be captured and kept them in zoos attached to their palaces.

In addition to his private pleasures, Mamun took part in the great communal holidays of the religious and secular calendars. To mark the end of the fast of Ramadan, military commanders and senior ministers staged elaborate processions, marching through the streets of Baghdad with their resplendently costumed followers. At the midwinter fire festival of Sadaq, the inhabitants of the city turned night into day, dancing on the riverbanks, traveling up and down the Tigris in gaudily decorated and illuminated boats—none so brilliantly adorned as those belonging to the caliph and the court.

In the spring the movement of the sun into the sign of Aries was marked by yet more public revelry during the six-day feast of Nawruz. People danced in the streets by the light of bonfires, perfumed their houses, exchanged presents, and sent one another greeting cards bearing good wishes. Loyal subjects from all walks of life lined up at the royal palace to shower their sovereign and his chief ministers with gifts. Pastry cooks brought delicacies, gardeners delivered the best fruits of the season, rug dealers presented their most dazzling carpets, poets offered specially written verses. And though he sat in a palace crammed with treasures, the caliph would have been scandalized if any courtier entered his presence without handing over a flask of incense or a particularly handsome jewel. "Where," he would inquire as guilelessly as a child at a birthday party, "is your gift of the day?"

Gift giving was also the order of the day on the occasion of Mamun's wed-

Accompanied by standard-bearers carrying banners with religious inscriptions proclaiming the greatness of God, a military band plays a fanfare to announce the end of Ramadan, the month of fasting. "Fasting," the prophet Muhammad once declared, "is one half of endurance." He then added, "Endurance is one half of the faith."

ding to Buran, the 18-year-old daughter of his vizier, or chief minister. On their wedding night, the couple sat on a mat made of gold, sapphires, and pearls, while hundreds more pearls—all of a prodigious size—rained down upon them. The most important guests were then wrapped in robes of honor, while the bride's father walked among them, scattering melon-sized balls of musk. Each ball contained a note with the name of a country estate, a slave girl, a fast horse, or some other valuable piece of property to be bestowed by the vizier upon the guest who received the ball. It was, beyond dispute, the wedding of the century.

Buran, sitting amidst her shower of pearls, harbored no illusions about her marriage to Mamun. There might be passion, love, and even friendship between her and her new husband, but she knew she would have to share him with a harem full of other women. And no matter how many sons she might bear him, she had

pleasures distract him from his higher purposes, though. His ambition was to consolidate and extend the powers of the caliphate, seeking to control not only the machinery of state but also the dogma of the faith itself. Two hundred years after its foundation, Islam was racked by a series of theological disputes and potential schisms. Believers argued bitterly over the Koran itself: Was it part of the divine essence, as eternal as the God whose mind it mirrored, or was it something that had been created, like the earth and everything on it?

Mamun espoused the doctrine that the Koran was a created thing. As caliph of the Islamic empire, he saw himself as heir to the Prophet's legacy. Therefore he claimed the authority to interpret the holy book as he saw fit. Most clerics were outraged by Mamun's bid to extend his power from the temporal into the spiritual realm and declared that they alone should control and interpret

"Chess and politeness do not go well together!"

no guarantee that he would name any of them as his successor.

Abbasid caliphs could have as many as four official wives and a seemingly endless supply of concubines. Some of the wives were the daughters of foreign chieftains or local dignitaries who wished to curry favor at court; the concubines might be prizes captured in war or slave girls purchased at the market. A caliph with a taste for variety might summon any passing slave who caught his eye—from a singer to a laundress—to share his bed. Some of these slaves, such as Mamun's chess-playing companion Arib, were well-educated and cultured individuals—poets, musicians, storytellers—whose talents had raised their market value to a price that few but caliphs could meet.

Mamun was far too ambitious a monarch to let domestic

religious law. Mamun responded by establishing an official inquisition, the *mihna*. Those clerics who repudiated the "createdness" doctrine would be banned from teaching and from praying in the mosque. Not even laymen were immune. Before a deceased person's relatives could claim their inheritance, they had to swear allegiance to the createdness doctrine. Judges tended to decide in favor of litigants who shared the caliph's views: In Egypt, a woman who sued for divorce won her freedom on the grounds that her husband opposed the creed.

Mamun might not tolerate dissent in theological matters that touched upon his political ambitions, but he engaged in open dialogue with scholars, astrologers, and scientists whose inquiries into the mysteries of creation sat uneasily with received religious truths. He invited men of ideas from all over the empire to debate subjects ranging from the relative merits of Christianity and Islam to the definition of love. Mathematicians, astronomers, engineers, and doctors of medicine all received generous grants from the caliphal purse.

But despite Mamun's curiosity, he did not approve of an experiment proposed by his personal physician, Yuhanna ibn Masawayh. The doctor had a son whose mental powers were extremely limited; he wished, in the interests of science, to cut him open and find out where nature had gone wrong. The horrified Mamun refused to allow it. Ibn Masawayh could hardly contain his frustration: "Had it not been for the meddling of the ruler and his interference in what does not concern him, I would have dissected alive this son of mine, just as Galen used to dissect men and monkeys. As a result of dissecting him, I would thus come to know the reasons for his stupidity, rid the world of his kind, and produce knowledge for people by means of what I would write in a book."

The caliph's admiration for the wisdom of the ancient Greeks caused him to commission translations of their great scientific and philosophical works. The Arabic versions of Aristotle, Euclid, Hippocrates, Plato, and Ptolemy created by Mamun's scholars preserved the legacy of classical learning for centuries to come. But Mamun's enthusiasm for the glories of Greece made him no more tolerant of the Greek-speaking Christians of the neighboring Byzantine Empire. In 830 he led an invading army into Byzantine territory, capturing towns and forts across Cappadocia in central Anatolia. In Mamun's view, his attacks on the Byzantines were no straightforward territorial struggle but an outright jihad—a holy war—to extend the dominion of Islam. When the harried Byzantine emperor Theophilos sued for peace, Mamun suggested he would consider it if Theophilos and all his subjects converted en masse to the faith of the Prophet. When Theophilos failed to respond, Mamun again went on the attack.

No matter how zealously he waged his holy war, Mamun would never be forgiven by his enemies in the religious establishment. On August 7, 833, during the campaign in Cappadocia, the 47-year-old caliph suddenly fell ill and died. Some of his followers believed his death had been caused by eating tainted dates; others claimed he'd caught a chill while crossing a frigid Anatolian mountain stream. But those who opposed the createdness doctrine disagreed. The 14th-century scholar al-Dhahabi, insisted Mamun had committed heresy and persecuted true believers. He deserved to be punished: "So God brought his end."

Less than 100 years after Mamun's death, another Islamic warrior was threatening Christian communities at the other end of the Mediterranean. On the morning of June 4, 920, a great army

assembled under the watchful gaze of amir Abd al-Rahman III, governor of the Muslim territories in Spain, which was known as Al-Andalus. The steely blue eyes of the amir missed nothing as his cavalrymen and foot soldiers mustered in the tens of thousands below the walls of the southern city of Cordoba, waiting for the order to march north and attack the Christians of León and Navarre.

Observing the sunlight flashing like diamonds off the points of well-polished spears, Abd al-Rahman seemed untroubled that the Christian blood he hoped to spill ran through the veins of his own relatives. For the amir of Al-Andalus was only one-quarter Arab: His paternal grandmother was a princess from the Basque kingdom of Navarre; his mother, a slave-concubine, came from the same mountainous region of northern Spain. Abd al-Rahman's fair complexion betrayed these origins, and to assert his Muslim identity he was said to have dyed his reddish beard and hair a more suitably Arab black.

The amir's army was composed of an even richer ethnic mix. Some of his men were the descendants of the conquering Muslim warriors of North Africa who had

A bearded Byzantine envoy receives instructions from his emperor, Theophilos, below right, then presents himself to Caliph Mamun, seated at left, in Baghdad. Envoys had to be particularly circumspect at the caliphal court. When one Byzantine representative delivered a letter to Mamun in which Theophilos was named before the caliph, Mamun returned the letter without reading it and used the insult as a pretext for war.

crossed the Strait of Gibraltar in 711 and made Spain the westernmost province of the empire. There were also soldiers whose ancestors had immigrated to Spain from Syria. But the Muslims in the army were rapidly being outnumbered by non-Muslims. Some of these new soldiers had enlisted as mercenaries, among them Christians from the north of Spain willing to fight on behalf of Islam as long as the price was right. Others were slave-conscripts imported from France, Italy, Greece, eastern Europe, and Africa. Most understood little Arabic and spoke even less, earning them the sobriquet "the Silent Ones."

Preparations for a military expedition took three to six weeks. The provincial governors—each one obliged to deliver a quota of fighting men on demand—needed time to marshal their forces and report to the royal encampment, just north of Cordoba. Here the soldiers would ready themselves for departure under the vigilant eye of the amir himself, who made a point of abandoning the comforts of the city to camp, alongside his men, in a temporary palace made of tents.

Abd al-Rahman knew he could rely on a meticulously organized war machine. The city's arms workshops turned out 3,000 tents and 1,300 shields annually, as well as 1,000 bows and 20 times that many arrows every month. Strings of war-horses, bred at stud farms along the Guadalquivir River, were led in from their pastures in the marshlands of Las Marismas; camels imported from Africa and mules from the Balearic Islands formed the baggage trains.

When setting off for war, the amirs of Al-Andalus valued ritual as much as logistics. Crowds lined the streets of Cordoba to bid farewell to their ruler as he departed, escorted by an imposing procession of armored warriors. Military flags were ceremoniously removed from the walls of Cordoba's Great Mosque, attached to the spears of the military chiefs, and carried out of the city in state. After the hostilities, the flags would be restored to their usual places within the sanctuary.

The campaign in that summer of 920 was all Abd al-Rahman had hoped for—and more. For three months his army rampaged through León and Navarre, sacking monasteries, churches, and settlements of all sizes. Burgos was burned, so too the nearby fortress of Osma. Once the amir's men had finished with it, according to one Muslim commentator, Osma resembled "a blackened piece of charcoal." Some prisoners, including two bishops, were held as hostages, but most were packed off for sale as slaves.

When Abd al-Rahman attacked the castle of Muez, its defenders—half dead of thirst in the baking summer heat—resisted him for four days. But his siege engines finally pounded the ramparts down. The men who had stood against him were decapitated on the spot; the amir wished to send their severed heads back home to Cordoba to hang as trophies on his city walls. This caused difficulties for the baggage train: There were more bloodstained bundles than the mules could carry.

The decisive victory against the Basque and Leónese forces came at Junquera, west of Pamplona. As the slave convoys shuffled south and the crows wheeled over the silent battlefield, Abd al-Rahman headed home in triumph. It had been a highly successful campaign. He not only had terrorized the infidels, he had also demonstrated his power to the rulers of the small independent Arab enclaves in the borderlands between Christian and Muslim territories.

Spain had first come under Muslim control during the early years of the eighth century, when the empire was still ruled by the Umayyad caliphs in Damascus. In 750, when the Abbasids deposed the Umayyads, the new caliph's uncle had invited 80 princes of the old ruling house to a peacemaking banquet. Just as the feast got under way, a gang of club-wielding assassins burst in and battered the guests to death. Leather covers were pulled

Victorious Muslim troops march homeward with Spanish Christian captives and their livestock in this 13th-century painting. The varied skin tones and hair color of the men in the cavalry and infantry reflect the multiethnic makeup of Muslim armies in Spain.

over the bodies of the dead and dying Umayyads, and the host and his other guests dined to the sound of the victims' groans.

One young Umayyad prince—the first Abd al-Rahman—managed to escape the slaughter. He fled to Egypt and across North Africa, with Abbasid henchmen hard on his heels. Only when he arrived in Spain—on the remote western edge of the Islamic world—did he feel himself safely out of reach of the Abbasids. Abd al-Rahman found other Syrian immigrants in Al-Andalus, and with their support he built a transplanted branch of the deposed Umayyad dynasty. No Abbasid armies came out of the east to challenge the new amir's autonomy; the distances were too great and the Abbasids themselves far too preoccupied with moving their base of operations farther east, to Iraq.

But even as the Umayyads consolidated their power over the local Muslim chieftains and confronted the Christians to the north, they mourned for their ancestral homeland. Abd al-Rahman I wrote poetry drenched in nostalgia and named his new summer residence al-Rusafa after the great Umayyad palace near Raqqa. Even those who had never set foot there clung to a romantic vision of life in the Arabic East.

In 822 a new immigrant from Baghdad brought a fresh and potent infusion of Eastern influences into Al-Andalus. At the time when Abd al-Rahman II—great-grandson of the first Abd al-Rahman—became amir, a musician formerly attached to the Abbasid court arrived in Cordoba. Ziryab was a gifted singer and *ud* player, master of a thousand Arabic songs, and an inspiring teacher. His greatest asset, however, was his ability to charm the new ruler and impress the upper classes.

The amir welcomed Ziryab into his intimate circle. He installed his new boon companion in a handsomely furnished mansion, showered him with gifts, and paid him a monthly salary. In exchange, Ziryab instructed his eager audience of provincial westerners in the latest modes and manners from Baghdad.

Cordoba's elite paid close attention to Ziryab—and to the increasing numbers of merchants and merchandise arriving from the East. They began to sport colorful silk gowns in springtime and subtly shaded quilted clothes in the fall. Men dyed their beards with henna and trimmed their locks to expose necks and ears. Both sexes discovered the delights of smelling sweet, rubbing their bodies with deodorizing unguents; cleaning their teeth with aromatic pastes; and sprinkling themselves, their houses, and their visitors with all kinds of perfumes.

Even dinner menus and table decorations altered in accordance with the dictates laid down by Ziryab. The rich sipped from crystal cups instead of quaffing their drinks from cumbersome golden goblets. They sampled such exotica as asparagus, which they soon began to grow at their own country estates. Culinary free-for-alls, where every dish arrived at once, gave way to an orderly sequence of courses, culminating in dessert.

By the time Abd al-Rahman III—the eighth Umayyad amir of Al-Andalus—came to power in 912, the people of Cordoba had shed their provincial inferiority complex. Their city had become the sophisticated center of a different world. It might lie on the frontier between Islamic civilization and the infidels, but in cultural terms it was a capital in its own right, no longer on the distant edge of anywhere.

Two intricately decorated stoppered perfume bottles, one silver and the other bronze, and a silk textile fragment attest to the sophistication of 10th-century Cordoba, the capital of Muslim Spain. The fragment's complicated design and abundant display of gold thread suggest that it was a product of the caliphal textile workshops.

Cordoba had become the jewel of Al-Andalus, the largest city on the Iberian Peninsula and, with an estimated 100,000 inhabitants, one of the largest cities in the Mediterranean world. Its magnificence dazzled contemporary visitors, such as the geographer Ibn Hawqal of Baghdad, who insisted that no place in North Africa, Egypt, or Syria could match "the size of its population, extent of its territory, area of its markets, cleanliness of its inhabitants, construction of its mosques, and number of its baths and hostelries."

Located on the banks of the Guadalquivir River, the city rose over an ancient bridge built by Roman engineers. Its seven-gated stone walls sheltered the amir's palace, the Great Mosque, the army barracks, various government buildings—including the mint—and the mansions of certain senior figures in the administration. Ibn Hawqal suggested that visitors climb the walls for an hourlong tour of the town. The view to the north was particularly pleasing. On this side of the city, extending toward the southern slopes of the mountains of Cordoba, lay

A Mosque on the Edge of Islam

Perhaps in response to the Prophet's promise that "God builds a house in Paradise for him who builds a mosque," the Syrian-born Abd al-Rahman I began construction in 785 of one of the architectural masterpieces of the Arab world, a place of worship he would call the Kaaba of the West, the Great Mosque of Cordoba.

Abd al-Rahman patterned his mosque after the grand Umayyad mosques of Syria and Palestine, re-creating their rectangular, arcaded prayer halls. In one respect, though, the Cordoba mosque may have imitated the Middle Eastern models too closely: Its qibla, the wall that is supposed to face Mecca to indicate the direction of prayer, faced south instead—the correct orientation for Damascus or Jerusalem but not for a city in Spain.

As Cordoba's population grew, the Great Mosque grew with it. Later rulers expanded its prayer hall, making the mosque the third largest in Islam. But the glory of the mosque —the shimmering mosaic decoration on the qibla and the main dome overhead—was the gift of Caliph al-Hakam II, son of Abd al-Rahman III, who supposedly brought a

mosaicist from Constantinople to work on it.

After the Christians reconquered Spain, the mosque remained relatively intact until Holy Roman emperor Charles V permitted the erection of a church on the site in the early 1500s. Upon seeing the church, Charles immediately regretted his decision. "You have taken something unique," he told the builders of the church, "and turned it into something mundane."

The solid walls and crenelated roof of the Great Mosque of Cordoba give the building a fortresslike aspect, appropriate for a mosque on Islam's frontier.

A forest of horseshoe-shaped arches fills the Great Mosque's vast prayer hall *(right)*. Many of the supporting columns came from Roman ruins, prompting the builders to use an ingenious two-tiered system of arches to compensate for the shortness of the scavenged columns.

Elaborate arches adorn the *maqsura,* an area of the mosque set aside for the ruler and his attendants. Located in front of the qibla—the wall facing Mecca—maqsuras were often enclosed to enhance the sovereign's status and security. At Caliph al-Hakam II's orders, the maqsura of the Great Mosque was rebuilt and beautified, then connected to the palace by a private passageway.

The artistic and spiritual focal point of the Great Mosque is its mosaic-encrusted mihrab *(left)*. A recess in the qibla wall that is supposed to be aligned with Mecca, the mihrab is where the prayer leader positions himself when directing worship.

Some of the gold mosaic cubes used in the dome at right, which rises above the maqsura, are said to have been a gift to al-Hakam from the Byzantine emperor in Constantinople.

residential neighborhoods, markets, workshops, suburban gardens, and—at a discreet distance from the noise and bustle of the town—the luxurious country mansions of the rich. The southern prospect, dominated by a cemetery and a leper colony, was less alluring.

Cordoba's cosmopolitan character was enhanced by the ethnic diversity of Al-Andalus: Residents included Arabs, Berbers from North Africa, Christians, native converts to Islam, and Jews, who had lived in Spain since Roman times. Each group influenced the others, and each had its own connections with the world outside. Muslims belonged to a spiritual and cultural commonwealth extending over three continents. Jews corresponded with fellow Jews in places as far off as India and regularly consulted the rabbinical academies in Iraq. And Christians looked to Rome for guidance.

Under Umayyad rule, Al-Andalus had waxed fat. Its merchants grew rich dealing in dried fruits, slaves, timber, furs, olive oil, and the remarkable wares produced by Cordoba's craftsmen: ivory boxes; creamy paper of the finest quality; the supple, ornately decorated crimson leather that would be called, after its place of origin, cordovan. Ships from Al-Andalus were a familiar sight in Mediterranean harbors all the way to Alexandria, and the region's traders could be found as far away as India and China. The traffic moved both ways: Drawn by the fame of its products, foreign merchants also made their way to Spain. After the secret of silk cultivation—along with the necessary worms—had been smuggled out of China and conveyed across the Islamic world, Al-Andalus became a major western center of production. For lovers of fashion, said Ibn Hawqal, Cordoba was the place to come for "precious garments of linen, cotton and silk."

The Umayyad rulers derived considerable profit from this commercial cornucopia, partly through tolls and tariffs, partly through the use of royal monopolies. Only the amirs, for instance, had the right to produce and distribute a distinctive fabric called

tiraz: Made of cotton or linen, each piece was embroidered with quotations from the Koran, the date it was made, its place of origin, and the name of the current ruler. But even a man as rich as Abd al-Rahman III could still be seduced by some well-chosen gifts. When he promoted his counselor Ahmad ibn Shuayd to an even more exalted post, the wealthy aristocrat expressed his gratitude with a fabulous quantity of gold and silver, furs from rare creatures such as the white fox of Khurasan, precious wood, 100 prayer rugs, 100 horses, ornate saddles and harnesses, tents, 60 slaves, and an assortment of miscellaneous trinkets.

Ahmad ibn Shuayd would certainly have been among the congregation that gathered for Friday prayers in the Great Mosque on January 16, 929. As the dignitaries of Cordoba assembled under the tall red-and-white banded arches of the prayer hall, there was a sense of expectation. As always, the amir and his entourage entered through a covered passageway that sheltered them from public view as they processed from the palace to their usual places within the sanctuary. In accordance with tradition, the weekly sermon began with a prayer acknowledging the ruler, but this time, the preacher hailed Abd al-Rahman III not as amir but as caliph—Commander of the Faithful.

These words must have been greeted with a most unliturgical rumble of excitement. The Umayyad amirs of Al-Andalus had often referred to themselves as "Sons of the Caliphs." Yet, like all Muslims, they had acknowledged that only the ruler of the Islamic empire could claim the title—even if he was, to their great irritation, an Abbasid. But Abd al-Rahman III had now decided that times were changing.

Vast distances did not prevent news from traveling swiftly across the Islamic world. It had become clear that the Abbasid caliphate was crumbling. Abd al-Rahman was not the only Muslim ruler who felt that the beleaguered monarch in far-off Baghdad no longer had the right to claim sovereignty over the entire community of believers. Across the Mediterranean Sea in Tunisia, the Fatimids, an Arab family whose ancestor had been a bitter rival of the earliest Umayyads, had already declared themselves caliphs.

Abd al-Rahman knew that the Fatimids were eager to extend their power farther into the North African territory called the Maghreb, a region of Umayyad influence and a vital channel for the imports of grain and gold required by Al-Andalus. To meet these challengers on equal terms, Abd al-Rahman decided that he had as much right as they did, if not more, to assume the status of caliph.

Abd al-Rahman III immediately sent a letter to all provinces announcing that he was now Commander of the Faithful. To mark the great day, he ordered his mint to produce an issue of gold dinars. These were the first gold coins to come out of Al-Andalus for 200 years; no northern European king would mint gold coins for another three centuries to come. The gold, from mines south of the Sahara, was a clear signal to followers and foes alike: The new caliph was as rich as he was powerful, and enemies would trifle with him—or his supply lines—at their peril.

Once he had established himself as caliph, Abd al-Rahman began to build a palace city far superior to the one that had suited him as amir. On a spit of land between two deep ravines, three miles west of Cordoba, he founded Madinat al-Zahra. According to some chroniclers, he named this new creation in honor of a favorite wife. But its site, its design, its furnishings, and every detail of its lavish and intricate decoration were chosen as a symbolic expression of the new caliph's absolute sovereignty.

Guarded by the sweep of sierra at its back, Madinat al-Zahra stood in lofty and solitary splendor, visible for miles and commanding an unbroken view of the countryside. Travelers from the east would recognize its intentional resemblance to certain old caliphal palaces in Iraq, placed on high ground to ensure that the ruler literally towered over his subjects and kept himself aloof from the mundane realities of the old capital nearby. But for all its resemblance in scale, design, and contents to the palace complexes of the Islamic East, Madinat al-Zahra displayed a character all its own.

Nothing like it had ever been seen before in the Western world. Madinat al-Zahra was no mere palace but an entire royal metropolis, with a mosque; a commercial quarter; government offices; gardens; and residences for the caliph, his court, his personal servants, and several thousand employees of the state. To increase the population there, he rewarded every new settler who built a house

some 6,000 stone building blocks each day, the project would not be entirely completed until 961.

In the meantime, al-Hakam was given a free hand by his father—and a generous, seemingly limitless, budget. In a typical year, as much as one-third of the state's revenues were spent on the building works, but there were also periods when the enterprise virtually drained the treasury. To create a capital on this previously empty hillside, al-Hakam's engineers built roads; terraced the slope; and devised a water supply system based on a large underground conduit, arched aqueducts, a water tower, a marble collection tank, and a complicated network of lead pipes. The palace and the homes of senior officials were equipped with running water, lavatories, bubbling fountains, and fishponds. Abd al-

"The hall sparkled with light and confounded all vision."

with a bounty of 400 silver dirhams.

The city's physical structure reflected the social order. The hillside site consisted of three great walled terraces. The lowest tier housed soldiers and ordinary workers, who lived alongside such necessary amenities as markets, bathhouses, and the mosque. The central terrace contained the residences of senior officials, as well as the office buildings where they worked. The uppermost level held the caliph's palace, rising high above the rest.

The making of Madinat al-Zahra was a massive project, personally supervised by Abd al-Rahman's son and designated successor, the future caliph al-Hakam II. Construction began around 936. The mosque was consecrated in 941, and by 946 Abd al-Rahman and his entourage were in residence, to be followed by the entire state administration, including the royal mint, in 947. But even with an army of as many as 10,000 laborers cutting

Rahman's own pools were so well stocked that it required 12,000 loaves of bread a day to feed their silvery and gold inhabitants.

Nothing was too good for Madinat al-Zahra, especially for the caliph's palace. No commonplace material would suffice when a rare and precious substitute could be found. To meet al-Hakam's high standards, the craftsmen of Al-Andalus outdid themselves in the creation of luxurious objects, while his agents scoured the world for foreign treasures.

More than 4,300 marble columns were collected from ancient Roman and Carthaginian sites. The principal reception hall featured a green marble basin from Constantinople that was encircled by 12 golden, jewel-encrusted sculptures spouting jets of water. Double doors of the finest wood gleamed with ebony and ivory marquetry; light glowed through windows of translucent alabaster. Curious mechanical devices—an automaton in the shape of a realistic lion, artificial songbirds, thrones that rose by means unseen into the air—dazzled and dumbfounded visitors.

The historian al-Maqqari, writing long after the palace had crumbled to dust, preserved the legacy of one particular reception hall, where a massive pearl hung from a ceiling of gold and marble. This pavilion, he recorded, "had eight openings formed by interlacing arches of ebony and ivory inlaid with gold and all manner of precious gems. The arches were supported on columns of colored marble and pure beryl. When the sun came through these openings and its rays rebounded off the roof and walls, the hall sparkled with light and confounded all vision."

Al-Maqqari also mentions a large pool filled with mercury. When Abd al-Rahman wanted to impress his guests, "he would signal one of his slaves to disturb the mercury. Then there would appear in the chamber a brilliancy like lightning which would fill their hearts with fear." This effect was exactly what the caliph had in mind. Whatever its other functions as royal residence or hive of bureaucratic industry, Madinat al-Zahra's main purpose was to inspire awe. And, in Abd al-Rahman's view, awe was an indispensable political tool, especially when dealing with foreign powers.

Ambassadors from alien kings were left with no doubt that Abd al-Rahman III was a ruler to be reckoned with. Their first intimation of his power came when they traveled from Cordoba to Madinat al-Zahra. As a foreign delegation walked out through the city gates, they found themselves ushered into a three-mile-long arched passageway composed entirely of soldiers standing shoulder to shoulder in two parallel lines, holding up huge swords that met, tip to tip, to form the roof. "The fear that this inspired," said the philosopher Ibn al-Arabi, "was indescribable."

Emerging from this tunnel of muscle and steel, the foreign diplomats passed through the gates of Madinat al-Zahra, only to find themselves greeted by an even more effective piece of theater. As they walked from the gates to the palace—over ground carpeted in silk brocade—they encountered a succession of imposing individuals in lavish costumes luxuriating on couches

Muslim scientists designed ingenious mechanical devices for the amusement of the royal court. In the example shown in the painting at left, wine drips into a tipping bucket that empties into a glass held by an automaton—a servant mounted on wheels inside a cabinet. The weight of the full glass causes the automaton to roll down the sloped floor, push open the door, and proffer the glass and a towel.

The Alhambra: Islam's Red Citadel

By the early 1200s, the mighty Umayyad dynasty of Al-Andalus had disappeared, and all that remained of Muslim Spain was the small Nasrid kingdom of Granada in the southeast. The Nasrids would seem to have little in common with their Umayyad predecessors. Whereas the Umayyads presided over a golden age in Al-Andalus, the Nasrid dynasty reigned during the time of the Christian reconquest of the peninsula. But in defiance of the advancing Christian tide, the Nasrids began to build a great palace city that would rival the glories of the Umayyad city of Madinat al-Zahra. It would be known as the Alhambra, the Red Citadel.

Erected on the slopes of the Sierra Nevada above the city of Granada, the Alhambra served as the capital of the Nasrid kingdom. Within its red clay walls, the Nasrids built mosques, villas, baths, a royal mint and cemetery, barracks, as many as six palaces, and elaborate waterworks that fed lush gardens and refreshing pools and fountains. The Alhambra also contained the homes and workshops of those who toiled in the royal city, which at its peak had a population of about 40,000.

The Nasrids decorated the Alhambra with some of Islam's most ornate interiors. Mainly using colored tile, wood, and plaster, master craftsmen covered every surface with designs of mesmerizing intricacy. In one especially magnificent hall, the domed ceiling seems to rotate slowly, an illusion caused by the play of light and shadow on its multifaceted decoration. Inscribed verses attributed to Muslim Spain's last great poet, Ibn Zamrak, ornament the palace rooms, many written as if the buildings themselves were addressing the viewer. "The stars would gladly descend from their zones of light," reads one verse, "and wish they lived in this hall instead of in heaven."

Stucco ornamentation of astonishing delicacy adorns the Alhambra's Lion Court, which takes its name from the 12 marble lions supporting the central fountain. The court and its adjacent halls served as a private retreat for the ruler.

Despite the imposing red clay walls and towers that gave the complex its name, the Alhambra fell to a Christian army without a struggle in 1492.

as handsome as thrones. "Each time the ambassadors saw one of these dignitaries," wrote Ibn al-Arabi, "they prostrated themselves before him, imagining him to be the Caliph, whereupon they were told, 'Raise your heads! This is but a slave of his slaves!'"

Finally they reached the inner sanctum to find a sight that, after all this splendor, was truly shocking. A gate opened to reveal a barren, sandy courtyard. According to Ibn al-Arabi, "At the center was the Caliph. His clothes were coarse and short: what he was wearing was worth no more than four dirhams. He was seated on the ground, his head bent; in front of him was a Koran, a sword and fire. 'Behold the ruler,' the ambassadors were told." After this, an emissary was putty in the caliph's hands.

Abd al-Rahman III was particularly pleased to receive a delegation from the Byzantine emperor in 949. He knew that a visit to Cordoba from the most important state in Christendom enhanced the caliphate's prestige on the international stage. No emperor would have deigned to send grandees bearing greetings and gifts to a humble amir. Some diplomatic missions were considerably less well received, however. When the Holy Roman emperor Otto I sent an ambassador in 956 to ask the caliph's help against Muslim pirates who were harrying settlements along the Rhone River, his chosen envoy did more to alienate Abd al-Rahman than to charm him. From the outset, the German monk John of Görz did not trouble to disguise his contempt for the Islamic faith; even before he met Abd al-Rahman in person, he managed to offend the caliph so badly that he was detained for several years in Cordoba, under a loose form of house arrest, before he was allowed to present Otto's petition. Only frantic behind-the-scenes diplomacy on the part of the bishop of Cordoba's Christian community prevented John from receiving the martyr's death he apparently desired.

The forbidding gateway below, known as the dark corridor, provided the only landward access to al-Mahdiyya, a coastal palace city in Tunisia built by the Fatimid rulers of North Africa. The Fatimids made a practice of building well-fortified royal residences to protect themselves from possible attack by their subjects.

Finally, Abd al-Rahman III agreed to meet the truculent Christian. But when the caliph sent messengers to him, John of Görz refused their request that he shave, bathe, and dress in clean clothes in preparation for his royal audience. Instead, he sent word to the caliph that as a monk he was not permitted to wear anything but his monastic habit. To the astonishment of his fastidious and well-scrubbed courtiers, Abd al-Rahman graciously conceded: "Even if he comes dressed in a sack, I will most gladly receive him."

When the day came for his reception, the caliph's troops put on their traditional, daunting martial display. But on this occasion, Abd al-Rahman did not present himself as a ragged ascetic, sitting on the ground with sword and Koran, but in the full splendor of an Islamic potentate, in a hall draped with the rarest silks and

Why, on such a bitter winter day, had the ruler summoned them all so urgently into his presence? And why had they been instructed to gather at one of the secondary gates, instead of the great portal used on state occasions?

As a servant led them through a maze of halls and passageways, their puzzlement increased. Then a set of doors opened to reveal a room lined and carpeted with plain felt mats. In its center the caliph, clad only in a simple tunic, sat cross-legged on the floor, leaning over a little writing desk, surrounded by piles of books. For a few moments, busy with ink and paper, he appeared oblivious to their presence. Then, with a final flourish of his pen and the satisfied sigh of one who has found the perfect phrase that has previously eluded him, the caliph looked up from his labors and greeted them.

"Dear brothers," he began, "this morn-

"Even if he comes dressed in a sack, I will most gladly receive him."

lined with lustrous tiles. Then the caliph amazed all onlookers by doing something he never did. He extended a hand for the monk to kiss and invited him to sit beside him. As if there had never been any ill-feeling between the two men, John agreed, and the mission proceeded to an amicable conclusion.

At the end of his long life, Abd al-Rahman would reflect that, in half a century's reign over Al-Andalus, he had experienced only two weeks that were entirely free of worry or care. The cause of some of those troubled days and restless nights was his Tunisian rival, the Fatimid caliph al-Muizz.

Buffeted by an icy wind, the Berber chieftains assembled outside Caliph al-Muizz's palace at Al-Mansuriyya. As they waited to be admitted, they greeted each other with curious glances.

ing, with such a winter cold, I said to the princes' mother . . . 'What do you think—do our brothers actually suppose that on such a day as this we eat and drink, loll about on costly pillows, covered in brocade and silk, and in fennec and sable fur, smelling of musk, drinking wine and singing, as do those who have their minds on this world?' Then it occurred to me to send for you, so that you might see with your own eyes how I behave when I am alone and removed from your gaze."

Apart from his wealth and his divine appointment, he was, the caliph explained, a man like any of them. He urged them to observe how busy he was, how pressed with the cares of government, how zealous in keeping up his official correspondence. And everything he did, he informed his visitors, he did for their benefit, to protect them, to increase their territories, and to confound their foes. So it would please him greatly if they would follow his example and, as he put it, "Do as I do when you are alone!"

The Berbers withdrew, suitably impressed. They were warriors, not scholars. But God had pleased to give them a learned ruler, one who wrote books as well as read them. When the burdens of state kept al-Muizz awake, he comforted himself by perusing the treasures in his library. And when he did sleep, he told his close companions, ancient authors such as Ptolemy visited him in his dreams.

Al-Muizz, who ruled North Africa from 953 to 975, was the fourth caliph of the Fatimid dynasty, which traced its ancestry back to the Prophet himself through his daughter Fatima. The Fatimids were Shiites, who believed that Muhammad's legitimate successors were the descendants of Fatima and her spouse, Ali, Muhammad's cousin. The claims of the Abbasid dynasty were therefore false; so too, said the Shiites, was Sunni Islam, the version of the faith espoused by those loyal to the Abbasids.

The Fatimids asserted that they alone possessed the divine right to rule the community of the faithful. Unlike the Sunnis, who came to view the caliph as a political leader only, the Fatimids believed their caliph was also the one true imam, or spiritual teacher, blessed with religious infallibility as well as absolute earthly power.

The Fatimids had first made their presence felt in the Islamic world in the 870s. They had emerged from southwestern Persia as leaders of a secretive missionary movement, the Ismailis. Ismailis blended revolutionary politics with spiritual redemption, predicting the arrival of a new messiah who would change the face of Islam beyond recognition: All believers would instantly apprehend the truth, eliminating the need for any religious laws or rituals.

An ivory casket that once belonged to the Fatimid caliph al-Muizz bears an inscription wishing God's blessings on him, "his fine ancestors, and his pure descendance." The Fatimids used the inscriptions on their coins, such as the gold dinars below, to signal their adherence to the Shia branch of Islam and reinforce their claim to the caliphate.

Despite persecution and forced migration, the Ismailis established a network of clandestine cells and secret agents throughout the Muslim world. By 909 they had succeeded in establishing their own caliphate and ruling an independent empire in North Africa. Its very existence was a slap in the face to the Abbasids, who were struggling to maintain their power back in Iraq.

Although they repudiated the Abbasids' caliphal authority, the Fatimids didn't hesitate to pay homage to their rivals' architectural achievements when building a palace city of their own. The great complex of Al-Mansuriyya, south of their Tunisian capital at Kairouan, took its design—a circular shape with the sovereign's palace at its heart—from the royal enclosure in the center of Baghdad.

Construction began during the caliphate of al-Muizz's father. In his youth al-Muizz had taken a keen interest in the building works; as caliph, he brought the project to completion. To provide the city with water, his engineers built an aqueduct, carried on tall stone arches, that came down from the mountains and ran for some 20 miles across the lowlands. It was, in the words of the caliph's friend and adviser, the qadi al-Numan, "an astonishing structure a full day's march in length!"

The qadi, or Islamic judge, was equally impressed by al-Muizz's new palace, a veritable tower of stone. But the crowning glory of Al-Mansuriyya, in al-Numan's eyes, was the awe-inspiring Great Hall, supported by two massive columns that al-Muizz's slave-soldiers had transported in a single day—"as swiftly as the wind and with no trouble"—from the old Roman ruins at Sousse.

The caliph was fascinated, even obsessed, by Roman remains. Once, he told al-Numan, while touring the ruins of Carthage, he had fallen asleep and received a visit from the prince who had built the city. They discussed warfare, religion, and other matters of mutual interest. The apparition then told al-Muizz, "I have been sent to you with instructions," and offered to answer any questions the caliph might have. "Then I fell silent and thought over what I might ask him, but he stood up and departed. Then I awoke."

Only a ghost would have dared make such a casual exit from al-Muizz's presence. Any mortal who had dealings with a caliph had to observe an elaborate protocol. On first entering the ruler's presence, individuals were compelled to prostrate themselves and kiss the ground. A precise etiquette governed the wording of salutations to the monarch and the gestures of respect required of those on different levels of the official hierarchy.

Courtiers knew the rules as well as they knew their own names; visitors learned fast. Anyone privileged to attend the caliph stood up straight, never twitched or fidgeted, kept silent unless directly addressed by him and then replied in a low but audible voice, and never laughed, even if the caliph himself—struck by something funny—was splitting his own sides. Some experts on court etiquette insisted visitors should not look directly at the monarch, but rather lower their gaze as a mark of humility and awe.

If the ruler invited someone to sit down in the royal presence, the lucky person was expected to adopt the correct position.

He had to keep his back straight, almost as if standing at attention, and should sit tentatively, without crossing his legs. Even members of the caliph's intimate circle—the nominated heir, other princes, the most senior members of his administration—had their prescribed positions in relation to the throne. Minor officials, who were too lowly to gain entry to the audience hall itself, were sometimes granted the privilege of crouching down to kiss the threshold.

The reverence accorded a caliph was extended to the objects he wore or carried as symbols of his authority. Al-Muizz's royal regalia included a parasol that shielded the ruler from the sun during formal processions and a jewel-topped turban made of special cloth that was wound around the royal head in a ritually prescribed manner by a single high-ranking servant.

Among the Fatimids, the aura of majesty surrounding the caliph-imam was particularly intense: As God's anointed, his person was sacred, and so too were the objects that he owned or touched. These articles possessed baraka, or grace, derived from their contact with the ruler and automatically transmitted to anyone who received them.

At banquets celebrating the New Year or the end of Ramadan, the caliph conferred baraka by distributing food to his subjects with his own hands; recipients would kiss the food and keep it, rather than eating it. His clothing was particularly prized by the bereaved, who begged the palace for castoff garments to use as funeral shrouds. Even the sight of the sovereign could transmit baraka: Troops bound for war were heartened to catch a glimpse of the ruler as they marched out through the gates of Al-Mansuriyya. Proximity to the caliph ensured receipt of his baraka, but he could also use this charismatic power to work miracles at a distance, healing the sick or bringing rain to a drought-stricken land.

To govern effectively, however, a caliph relied on his trusted advisers even more than he did on his baraka. A key member of al-Muizz's inner circle was Jawhar, a former slave who had been freed by the caliph's father. He was known as "the Slav" but may have been of Italian origin; he had passed through the hands of various owners, including two highly placed eunuchs, before being presented as a gift to al-Muizz's father. Once liberated, Jawhar continued to serve at court. He had the title of *katib*, or secretary, but his role under al-Muizz was that of a senior minister, responsible for issuing all official documents and decrees. And when the time came for the Fatimid army to go to war, Jawhar became al-Muizz's most successful general.

In the course of his 22-year-long caliphate, al-Muizz transformed the Fatimid empire into a redoubtable international power. His armies, under the command of Jawhar, rode roughshod over the fiercely independent tribes of Algeria, putting virtually all of North Africa under Fatimid control. In 959 Jawhar reached the Atlantic coast of Morocco. As a souvenir from the very edge of the known world, he sent his master a gift of ocean fish kept alive in salt water.

These movements had not gone unnoticed in Cordoba. There were powerful strategic and economic motives for keeping northwestern Africa under Umayyad control. A Fatimid army wetting its collective feet in the Atlantic was not a comfortable prospect for the ruler of Al-Andalus. Umayyad forces had succeeded in defending their Moroccan garrisons at Ceuta, Tangier, and Sala but failed to hold out against Jawhar's prolonged siege of their vital stronghold at Fez.

By this time the Umayyads in Cordoba had long since abandoned any pretense of Muslim solidarity. In the mid-950s they forged an alliance with the infidels of the Byzantine Empire, who were equally alarmed by al-Muizz's threat to the balance of power in the Mediterranean. Eventually the Byzantines weakened and negotiated an armistice with the Fatimid foe. Al-Muizz took control of the island of Sicily and accepted annual tribute from Constantinople; in exchange he promised

Young boys undergo the rite of circumcision during a circumcision festival in 1582 in honor of a 16-year-old Turkish prince. Most Muslim circumcisions were carried out when the boys were 13, marking their passage to manhood.

to leave the Byzantine colonies on the Italian mainland undisturbed.

By the spring of 962, al-Muizz was in a triumphant mood. He had brought his dynasty to the height of its power, put down rebellions, and confounded his foes. He had also arrived at a joyous landmark in his personal life—the time when his own three sons would undergo the sacred rite of circumcision. The caliph-imam sent word to all parts of his dominion, summoning every Muslim family with sons due for initiation to manhood to a month-long, empire-wide circumcision festival. Each boy—rich or poor, nomad or city-dweller, Sunni or Ismaili—would receive money and gifts; families that refused to participate would be penalized.

Al-Numan and his fellow advisers calculated the number of boys involved and blanched at the likely cost to the caliphal purse. But al-Muizz would not be dissuaded. He saw the event as a momentous act of unification, bonding all the Muslims of his realm, no matter which sect they belonged to, into a single Islamic community guided by the one true imam.

The festival took place in the Islamic month of Rabi al-Awwal, which that year fell between April 8 and May 7. Tens of thousands of children were brought to Al-Mansuriyya by their parents and lined up outside the palace gates to wait their turn. Once admitted into the great courtyard, they entered one of the tented pavilions, where a brigade of trained circumcisers worked from early morning until dusk. Parents embraced their screaming sons, soothed their wounds with aromatic oils, and poured rose water on their heads. Acrobats and entertainers, specially imported from northern India, performed every trick they knew to distract the boys.

According to al-Numan's records, between 5,000 and 10,000 boys were circumcised daily. On the festival's final day, 12,000 came forward, with 300 latecomers admitted—by the caliph's gracious permission—on the following morning. As an army of slaves dismantled the pavilions, al-Muizz declared the event a political and personal triumph.

Seven years later al-Muizz would receive additional proof of his great destiny. On February 6, 969, he rode out from Al-Mansuriyya to watch General Jawhar lead the Fatimid army east out of Tunisia toward Egypt. Both caliph and general knew that Egypt—which was ruled by a family of amirs on behalf of the Abbasids in Baghdad—was ripe for an easy conquest. It had recently been visited by a series of catastrophes reminiscent of the biblical plagues of Egypt: drought, famine, infestations of rats, swarms of locusts. At al-Muizz's behest, Ismaili agents had prepared the ground, persuading the population that any hope for a better life lay with the Fatimid caliph-imam. The merchants of Fustat, it was whispered in that city's bazaars, were prepared to welcome an invasion with open arms.

When Jawhar's troops arrived in the Nile delta, they found a delegation of religious and secular leaders waiting to greet them. On July 6 the Fatimid army took bloodless possession of this easternmost addition to their empire. The Egyptians found the tenor of their lives relatively undisturbed by the new regime. Their own efficient and long-established state bureaucracy remained in place, and no pressure was put on them to forsake their Sunni creed.

On the site that would later become the city of Cairo, just northeast of Fustat, Jawhar immediately began constructing a royal complex to equal Al-Mansuriyya. In accordance with al-Muizz's wishes, he would serve there for four years as viceroy, while the caliph-imam prepared to move the seat of the Fatimid empire from Tunisia to Egypt.

In November 972 the inhabitants of the old Tunisian capital of Kairouan solemnly lined the road that led to Al-Mansuriyya to view an extraordinary spectacle. A seemingly endless baggage train, composed of donkeys and camels, emerged from the gates of the city. The beasts of burden staggered under the weight of silk hangings, carpets, chests of books and documents, baskets, and bundles all carefully sealed to protect their contents from dust. Behind them, heavily guarded, came animals bearing the entire royal treasury, which had been melted down into gold and silver bars for easier transport. These worldly goods were followed at a suitable distance by a procession of Fatimid dignitaries mounted on horses and camels and accompanied by their wives, children, and concubines, all shielded from sight in curtained litters.

The onlookers, murmuring among themselves, fell silent when the caliph-imam, sheltered by his royal parasol, rode by. They reached out their hands as if to draw every possible scrap of his baraka into themselves, wondering if good fortune—like their ruler—would now desert them for a new promised land in the east. Their hearts sank even further when they saw the lavishly draped litters bearing the coffins of the three previous Fatimid caliphs, who had built and ruled their empire from Kairouan.

It would take the caliph-imam's caravan more than six months to travel along the coast from Kairouan to Alexandria in Egypt; meanwhile, the Fatimid fleet made a parallel journey by sea. On June 10, 973, al-Muizz made his formal entrance into his new capital, Cairo. He would die there 18 months later, secure in the knowledge that his own dynasty had entirely eclipsed the Abbasids as the dominant power in the Islamic world. Even in the very heartland of the faith, in the holy cities of Mecca and Medina, Friday prayers would now culminate in a blessing upon the caliph in Egypt, instead of the caliph in Baghdad.

A Love Affair with Style

"The beauty of man," says a Bedouin maxim, "lies in the eloquence of his tongue." Those words reflect the passionate belief that made literature one of the Arab world's most original achievements, and one of the hardest for non-Arabic-speaking people to enjoy. For with few exceptions, Arabic poetry and prose were meant to be recited; content had less value than style, which strove for concision and clarity and exploited the musical rhythm of Arabic in ways no translation could capture.

A Thousand and One Nights, that patchwork quilt of Persian, Indian, and Arabic folklore whose genies and magic carpets became wildly popular in the West, never won similar acclaim in the Arabic-speaking world. The prose was too inelegant. "A vulgar, insipid book," one Arab critic called it. If westerners considered it the treasure of the Arabic tongue, Arabic speakers themselves reserved such status for the Koran and, second only to that, the 12th-century *Maqamat* of al-Hariri.

In al-Hariri's collection of picaresque adventures, the story is simply a pretext for verbal acrobatics, puns, riddles, sly allusions, and clever metaphors. One entire episode is created solely out of undotted and unjoined Arabic words. Abu Zayd, the wily hero of the *Maqamat*, is pictured here showing off his literary ingenuity before a captivated crowd, who will reward him for his wit with money.

Because Islam discouraged figural representation, illumination did not appear in literary manuscripts until the 11th century, and still there was some reluctance about painting live people. The figures in this miniature were later symbolically slain by drawing a slash over them, rendering the image theologically correct.

Poetry before the Prophet

Arabic literature was born on the sandy plains of central and northeastern Arabia, where nomadic tribes led a hardscrabble, monotonous life enlivened by participation in frequent raids. Each tribe had a poet who was inspired, it was thought, by jinns and who served as the tribe's entertainer and propagandist. In addition to regaling their tribes with verses, these Arabian bards flexed their verbal muscles at intertribal poetry tournaments, where they eloquently glorified the deeds of warrior kinsmen and bitterly denounced the enemies of their people.

Around AD 500, poets began singing qasidas, or long odes. These odes consisted of three loosely connected parts: a prologue lamenting the loss of a lover whose tribe has moved away, a journey through the desert, and either a eulogy glorifying the poet's tribe or invective aimed at the tribe's enemies. Seven of the most celebrated qasidas were collected during the eighth century under the title *Muallaqat;* because the word means "suspended poems," a legend arose that the prizewinning works were transcribed on fine linen and hung in the Kaaba at Mecca. With elaborate meter schemes, monorhyme, and a genius for capturing sharp images in a few precise words, as reflected in the quoted passage at right, the *Muallaqat* set the poetic standard for centuries to come.

One of the *Muallaqat*'s seven poets, Antarah, is pictured here in two guises: on the left as a revered wordsmith and on the right as a legendary Arab folk hero, the Black Warrior, returning from battle.

The bittersweet aspects of love often were an integral part of the qasidas. In the painting below, illustrating a Turkish love poem, lovers in a tent bid farewell before a long separation.

I split through his shielding armor
with my solid lance
(for even the noblest is not sacrosanct
to the spear)
and left him carrion for the wild beasts
to pounce on,
all of him, from the crown of his head
to his limp wrists.

The lion tears his friend the bull to pieces while the jackals Kalila and Dimna look on. The lion, ruler of his kingdom, will later learn that he has been duped by the envious Dimna into thinking his friend was false. The warning to princes: Be circumspect about taking advice from subjects.

Crows flap their wings to fan the flames that will suffocate owls trapped in a cave. Earlier, the owls captured a crow; after waiting patiently, the hostage won his release, then rallied fellow crows to exact vengeance. The moral: Forbearance in the presence of your enemies pays off.

Fables to Enlighten and Amuse

In the mid-eighth century, the heart of Islam shifted from desert Arabia to urban Baghdad, enriching Arab thought with fresh influences and ushering in a golden age of literature. For approximately a hundred years, Arabic prose had been confined to the mesmerizing language of the Koran, the inimitable Word of God. Now life in the city fostered the development of a secular type of prose that combined practical advice with entertainment. Manuals, romances, and tales—collectively known as *adab*—instructed princes and bureaucrats in the art of living and became immensely popular throughout the new urban society.

The first adab was written by Ibn al-Muqaffa, a Persian convert to Islam known for his translation of Indian fables under the title *Kalila and Dimna*. In it the philosopher Bidpai grooms a king to rule by recounting a string of fables featuring two jackals—worldly-wise Kalila and his treacherous brother Dimna—and a veritable caravan of talking monkeys, crows, camels, fleas, and other animals.

Appearing around 750, *Kalila and Dimna* was one of the few Arabic masterpieces to be copiously illustrated. The stylized paintings here, 14th- and 15th-century works that reflect the tales' enduring popularity, each embody a moral lesson from one of the fables.

To save the hares' water hole from thirsty elephants, the clever hare Fayruz tricks an elephant king into thinking that the moon has ordered him to depart. The lesson: Gullibility breeds losers.

Primers in Rhyming Prose

In the 10th century, libraries and universities began springing up across the Muslim world; at the same time, paper became increasingly available. These events ushered in the full flowering of Arabic literature. Over the next two centuries, an elaborately wrought form of rhymed prose developed to which the Arabic language was uniquely suited.

Following the style of the Koran, which uses rhyme, the storyteller al-Hamadhani, known as "the Wonder of the Age," invented a genre called *maqama*, an Arabic word referring to a literary gathering. In the *Maqamat* by al-Hamadhani, a scheming vagabond pops up at such gatherings and mesmerizes audiences with his word juggling and satirical takes on contemporary manners.

Al-Hamadhani's antihero was a model for Abu Zayd, the charming swindler who appears in al-Hariri's 12th-century *Maqamat.* Its grammatical sophistication was so esteemed that children of the elite who had already mastered the Koran often memorized passages from it. Such students were encouraged in their endeavors by an abundance of illustration rarely seen in literary manuscripts.

After drugging al-Harith's wedding guests, a destitute Abu Zayd robs them and passes the stolen goods to his son. According to the text of the maqama, this outrageous but seductive swindler then recites an enchanting poem to win al-Harith's forgiveness.

Before departing for Mecca, Abu Zayd affectionately embraces al-Harith, the narrator of al-Hariri's *Maqamat.* Their repeated encounters form the framework of this picaresque adventure written in rhyming prose.

A 13th-century miniature illustrates an episode from al-Hariri's *Maqamat* in which Abu Zayd and al-Harith sail to the Eastern Isles, which are inhabited by a harpy and other exotic creatures.

CHAPTER THREE

"THE GARDEN OF THE WORLD"

The hustle and bustle of this 19th-century Cairo street scene would have seemed familiar to residents traveling on the narrow thoroughfares of medieval Cairo. "I went through the streets of this city," wrote the noted 14th-century historian Ibn Khaldun, "which were choked with throngs of pedestrians, and through its markets, which overflowed with all the delights of life."

 For several days now, Ibn Ridwan, one of Cairo's leading physicians, had been suffering from severe headaches. A confirmed disciple of the ancient Greek physician Galen, the Muslim doctor diagnosed his pain according to Galenic theory: namely, that it was the result of an imbalance in one of the four bodily humors—blood, phlegm, yellow bile, and black bile. These humors, Galen taught, affected not only physical well-being but also psychological temperament, making some people sanguine, for instance, others phlegmatic, and still others choleric. In this case, Ibn Ridwan concluded, the throbbing in his temples stemmed from "an overfilling of the blood vessels of the head." In an effort to restore equilibrium by reducing the excess, Ibn Ridwan performed a venesection, a drawing of blood from a vein. Although he repeated the procedure several times, the headaches stubbornly persisted.

Then one night the ailing doctor saw Galen in a dream. As Ibn Ridwan later recounted in one of his many treatises, "He asked me to read to him his *Methodus medendi*. I read to him seven parts of it, and when I reached the end of the seventh part, he said to me: 'Here! I forgot the kind of headache from which you are suffering.'" At this point in the dream, Galen prescribed "cupping"—drawing blood to the skin's surface by applying a glass or metal cup from which the air has been drawn—at the base of the skull. "I awoke and did the cupping," Ibn Ridwan wrote, "and got rid of the headache on the spot."

That a Muslim physician in the mid-11th century should obey the dream instructions of an ancient Greek was not as unusual as it might seem. By Ibn Ridwan's time, numerous scholars had translated much of the philosophic and scientific literature of ancient Greece into Arabic, the language of the Islamic empire. In so doing, they built an intellectual and scientific foundation that would give rise to an age later viewed as the Renaissance of Islam. During this period, Egypt—and especially its capital, the twin cities of Fustat-Cairo—enjoyed a growing population, a flowering of artistic creativity, and widespread economic prosperity.

Such prosperity benefited Muslim and non-Muslim alike, as evidenced by the life and fortunes of Ibn Ridwan's contemporary, the Jewish merchant-banker Nahray ben Nissim. Nahray, an immigrant to Fustat-Cairo from Tunisia in the Maghreb, was involved in the exchange of all sorts of goods, including textiles, a trade that flourished under the Fatimid dynasty. With their dominion reaching east from Egypt into Arabia and Syria and west across North Africa, the Fatimids were ardent promoters of expanding international trade, not only throughout the vicinity of the Mediterranean and the Red Sea but also as far away as Europe and India. With gold flowing into Egypt from Nubian mines and with the caliph's treasury well filled with revenues from taxes and tribute, the Fatimid court spurred the development of other luxury items as well, including glass and ceramics. As a key distribution center for all these goods, Fustat-Cairo grew in stature, and a succession of caliphs built lavish palaces and beautifully appointed mausoleums and mosques.

Sitting by his booth, a cupper prepares to treat a patient by pressing a heated vessel onto the man's skin, a procedure thought to have healing and detoxifying effects. The features of the patient in this painting reflect the Far Eastern influences that began to appear in Syrian and Egyptian art after the Mongol invasion of the 13th century.

Fatimid patronage also fostered a high degree of intellectual activity, especially in the fields of philosophy, religion, and science.

From this high-water mark, the dynasty soon would weaken and eventually fall. Factional strife within the Muslim empire and incursions into Islamic territory by Christian crusaders and the Mongol warriors of Genghis Khan all took their toll. Ultimately, in the 13th century, a new militaristic regime known as the Mamluks gained ascendancy. Somehow Fustat-Cairo survived these long years of upheaval, becoming by the late 14th century one of the Muslim world's great educational centers. Renowned as a forum for public lectures and disputations, the city drew eminent scholars such as Ibn Khaldun, a noted historian, jurist, and diplomat who immigrated to Egypt from Tunisia in 1382.

Ibn Khaldun shared with Ibn Ridwan and Nahray ben Nissim a deep understanding of their city on the Nile. As a physician, Ibn Ridwan would dedicate himself to preserving and restoring the health of his fellow Cairenes. Nahray ben Nissim, though he always thought of himself as a Maghrebi, would live more than 50 years in his adopted home, coping with the hazards of international trade and establishing himself as a respected community leader. And Ibn Khaldun, another Maghrebi, would serve the Mamluk ruler in Cairo for more than two decades, capping an eventful career by meeting outside the gates of Damascus with the great conqueror Tamerlane. He then returned to Cairo to live the remainder of his days in the city he called "the metropolis of the universe, the garden of the world."

Cairo would eventually be worthy of the accolades that Ibn Khaldun bestowed on it, but its twin city, Fustat, was the thriving urban center in the 11th century, when the physician Ibn Ridwan practiced. Fustat grew on the site of an earlier military encampment, and its name may be derived from the Arabic word for tent or from the Greek word for the type of tents that were pitched by the Islamic army when they captured a Byzantine fortress on the Nile in the seventh century. Located at the apex of the river's vast delta, the encampment site was safe from seaborne attack and had easy access to Egypt's wealthy interior. The strategic location led Islamic rulers to transfer the capital there from Alexandria, a Mediterranean seaport west of the Nile. Late in the 10th century, the Fatimid caliph al-Muizz decided to create a royal refuge northeast of Fustat and established Cairo, a city that would eventually merge with Fustat and come to rival Baghdad itself. Fustat, meanwhile, continued to expand, with buildings up to seven stories tall and, according to one visitor, "large open spaces, enormous markets, impressive commercial centers" and "flowering gardens and parks that are always verdant, whatever the season."

Among the institutions that would contribute to Cairo's burgeoning intellectual reputation was the Dar al-Ilm, or House of Knowledge, established in 1005 by Caliph al-Hakim. Modeled after a similar institution in Baghdad, the House of Knowledge was stocked, as one contemporary chronicler wrote, with all the books the caliph deemed essential: "that is, the manuscripts in all the domains of science and culture, to an extent to which they had never been brought together for a prince." The doors of the Dar al-Ilm were open to people from all walks of life, who could come to read books or to copy them—with paper, reed writing implements, ink, and inkstands all donated by the caliph himself.

No doubt Ibn Ridwan studied there, for the learning necessary to become a physician required heroic effort. The son of a poor baker in Giza, a district across the river from Fustat, Ibn Ridwan noted in his autobiography that the astrological signs at his birth suggested that he should pursue medicine. This was not a simple undertaking. After moving to the capital at the age of 10, he began to study medicine and philosophy at 14. Without other financial support, he eked out a living by practicing astrology, substituting at a friend's medical office, and giving lessons to other students. But the aspiring doctor was soon dis-

why, the doctor replied that he wanted to look older so that people would respect him more as a doctor. Ibn Ridwan chastised the man and sent him on his way. Another physician, so refined that he always rode his mule with a pillow placed between his seat and the saddle, refused to consider a patient's illness until he had consulted an astrolabe, presumably because the position of the sun would influence the course of treatment. Still another prescribed "the dripping of milk on his head on very cold days" for a man who was paralyzed on one side of his body.

Quick as he was to condemn what he considered quackery in others, Ibn Ridwan was not without his own blind spots and pet theories: In one of his treatises, he dealt with the subject of "the protection of hot-tempered people against the harmfulness of sweets." Still, Ibn Ridwan was a conscientious doctor. "When you are called to a patient," he once wrote, "give him at first harmless remedies until you know his disease, then begin the real treatment." Imbued with Galen's theory that everything in nature was under the influence of the four humors, Ibn Ridwan believed that to know the disease, the doctor had to identify which bodily humor was the source of the trouble and then find a way to restore the necessary balance between the body and its environment. Convinced that "Egypt and everything in it are weak in their substance," he rejected the drugs and other remedies prescribed in medical books by the Greeks and Persians as being "aimed at bodies with strong constitutions and coarse humors." Instead, he believed that treatment "should be adapted to the bodies in Egypt."

Ibn Ridwan thus advocated the careful use of gentle drugs and moderate dosages for his patients. One of his prescriptions for strengthening the stomach, for example, was composed of a combination of sour quince juice, sour apples, acrid wine, and sweet and sour pomegranates blended with ginger, musk, saffron, and other spices. Another, rather tasty-sounding drink designed to preserve the body "in the time of a pestilence" was made of white wine or sweet basil juice and the

The people of medieval Cairo stored drinking water in jars like the marble one at left. They also used earthenware jars, which often had filters baked into their necks to trap insects *(above)*.

Richly patterned and colored garments, black veils of delicate weave, and hands and fingernails decorated with henna mark these Arab women as ladies of fashion.

juices of sour quince, apple, citron, and sweet and sour pomegranates, boiled and drunk with a sweetened syrup.

In time, the doctor's diligent work won him appointment as chief physician of Egypt by Caliph al-Mustansir. He also acquired sufficient wealth to marry, start a family, and purchase several substantial properties throughout Fustat, then the capital's commercial heart. No doubt he rode through the city to make his rounds, rather than traveling on foot. After passing through the narrow streets on hot summer days, Ibn Ridwan must have returned home grimy with the dust that rose from the region's powdery soil and hung in the still air. All day his senses would have been assaulted by the stench of animal droppings, open sewers, and latrines emptying into the Nile. Not surprisingly, pestilence and epidemics occurred with some frequency.

Purifying water for drinking would have been one of the major domestic tasks of Ibn Ridwan's wife, or at least of one of the household slaves. Her husband, of course, had precise recipes for purifying water according to the temperament of the individual and the time of year. In summer, for instance, irascible people were instructed to use a combination of vinegar, Armenian clay, red earth, chalk, and various crushed spiny shrubs. In winter, those of more placid temperament were to filter their water with the pith of apricot pits, dill, wild thyme, and bitter almonds. After such treatments, the water would be further clarified through several repetitions of skimming, heating, and letting it sit overnight before it was deemed fit to drink.

If it was a Thursday, the eve of the Muslim Sabbath, Ibn Ridwan's wife might well have been looking forward to one of the essential pleasures of an Egyptian woman:

Working Women

Muslim women had a wide range of professional options, among them scholarship, philanthropy, domestic work, commerce, medicine, or midwifery. Mostly, however, they were expected to have dealings only with other women, ideally within the confines of their own homes.

As in other societies, career paths were determined by social class. A woman who inherited her father's estate, for example, could buy and sell property, invest in trade, or lend money at interest. Wealthy upper-class women might endow the arts, commission a new mosque, or study with renowned scholars.

Women of all classes learned to sew, as well as to spin, dye, and card silk, cotton, and linen. Production of textiles was a lucrative cottage industry for middle-class women. But because they could not trade openly in the marketplace, they had to hire middlemen to sell their goods. Lower-class women often had to seek less desirable positions outside the home, working as bath attendants, hairdressers, teachers, and entertainers. The unskilled washed the dead and served as professional mourners at funerals, while the desperate were forced into slavery or prostitution—an occupation, one male scholar reflected contemptuously, "despised by scholars and better people."

Weaving was a profitable career option for middle-class Muslim women. At right, a woman spins thread, using one hand to turn the wheel's handle and the other to steady the bobbin of thread.

Assisted by servants, a midwife attends a wealthy woman during a difficult birth while the husband *(top, middle)* and other family members occupy themselves elsewhere. The midwife was an honored professional who was allowed to practice outside her home.

Female performers often entertained guests at wedding feasts. In the celebration shown at right, a group of Indian Muslim women dance, play castanets, and beat tambourines; men blow trumpets and bang on drums.

a weekly visit to the public bath. Many considered this ritual vital to a woman's mental as well as physical health. But not everyone considered Fustat's more than 50 bathhouses to be a blessing: Ibn Ridwan, for one, complained that the excessive smoke from the bathhouses' large hearths polluted the air.

During the rest of the week, Ibn Ridwan's wife would have performed her ablutions in her own washroom. A servant would help her each morning, dipping the ewer into a copper basin and pouring water over her mistress's hands. For soap, she would have used *ushnan,* pulverized ashes, scooped from a brass box. Around her on the dressing table there would be a silver mirror and a jewelry box, perhaps made of sandalwood and adorned with silver filigree. After applying kohl to her eyes and running a silver comb through her hair, she would have mixed and applied fragrant perfumes from a silver vessel.

Once ready to begin her day, Ibn Ridwan's wife—or her slaves—would have faced a number of duties, for her husband was a man with definite ideas. From air quality to diet to housekeeping, Ibn Ridwan adhered to the Galenic ideal of balanced temperaments and humors. Thus, in summer, his wife probably used a combination of flowers, water, fans, and fumigants to cool and freshen the air, making a special effort to place

cooling aromatics such as violets, roses, and wild thyme in the living room. On cold days, she might have set vases of sweet basil, narcissus, and lily of the valley to warm on stoves placed in the living quarters. In winter, thick carpets imported from Damascus and Iraq would have covered the floors, replaced in summer by reed mats. Ibn Ridwan's dietary edicts also varied according to the season. On a typical summer evening, his wife might prepare a meal of lamb, spinach, cucumber, and barley. In winter, the fare would likely have featured heavily spiced sparrow meat, beets, chickpeas, asparagus, garlic, leeks, onions, and fennel. Regardless of the season, however, Ibn Ridwan declared that food should be prepared "in a way that is agreeable to the body of the eater and to the type of food that is eaten."

Rather than cook an entire meal, Ibn Ridwan's wife might, on occasion, have asked her husband to stop at the

A jeweler, an apothecary, a butcher, and a baker ply their trades in shops lining a street in a covered market, known as a suk. The "hole in the wall" stalls were typical of medieval Islamic suks, although vendors of the same commodity usually congregated in the same area.

bazaar on his way home. Ibn Ridwan would likely have visited the shop of a *harras,* a specialist in preparing *harisa,* the medieval version of hamburger—a combination of ground meat and wheat fried in fat. From other shops would come groats cooked with dates, a cold relish, vinegar sauce, and bread; for dessert, he might pick up a sweet known as *qataif,* which was made of flour and almonds. Ibn Ridwan would have resisted the temptation to snack on the food in the bazaar, though; eating in public was considered improper and not something respectable citizens would ever do.

After dinner Ibn Ridwan might spend the rest of the evening devoting himself to what he called his "main recreation"—"the thought of God and His praise." Reclining against bundles of textiles on the carpet-covered floor, he would read through the pages of the Koran, dipping from time to time into the works of Plato and Aristotle. But the good doctor did not always maintain this aura of peaceful contemplation. Competition among Cairo's many practicing physicians was fierce, and Ibn Ridwan had a particular rival in a certain Ibn Butlan, a well-known Christian doctor from Baghdad who had arrived in Cairo in 1049.

To anyone but two men as opinionated and contentious as this pair, the source of the controversy between them—the question of whether a chicken or a young bird of any other species is more warm blooded—might have seemed trivial indeed. On a deeper level, however, the argument was really over which man could claim to be better educated in classical learning. For Ibn Ridwan, who considered himself "humble, sociable," and "devoted to godliness," the controversy seems to have led to phenomenal heights of venom and outrage. When one of Ibn Ridwan's houseguests declared of Ibn Butlan's treatise on the matter, "By Allah, he who utters such opinions is a liar," Ibn Ridwan gleefully recounted how he and his other guests "all laughed heartily about it."

The dispute could sometimes be comical. Ibn Ridwan, for

example, issued a barrage of pamphlets with such titles as "Discourse on the astonishing things alleged by Ibn Butlan" and "Discourse on the fact that Ibn Butlan does not understand his own sayings and still less those of others." Ibn Butlan, in turn, relished visions of Ibn Ridwan's patients complaining to God on Judgment Day about their wrongful death at Ibn Ridwan's hands. At other times, the feud descended into cruelty. Ibn Butlan once wrote a rhyme about Ibn Ridwan's being so ugly that the midwives at his birth wished they had left him in the womb. Ibn Ridwan, for his part, encouraged other Cairo physicians to join in ridiculing his rival, "to laugh at him and to avoid speaking with him." This tactic seems to have been the last straw: In 1052 Ibn Butlan left Cairo. Eventually he settled in Antioch, Syria, where he became a monk. As an antagonist, if not necessarily as a classicist, Ibn Ridwan had emerged the clear victor.

Even as Ibn Ridwan was tending the ill and feuding with his rival, Nahray ben Nissim was doing his part to maintain Egypt's mercantile trade. After several years of commuting between Fustat and his homeland in Tunisia, Nahray settled in Egypt in about 1050 and married a Fustat girl from an influential Jewish family. Over the next half-century, he would thrive as a merchant-banker and scholarly leader of Fustat's Jewish community.

In keeping with custom, Nahray and his bride lived with her family, moving into an apartment in a mansion owned by her two brothers. A house such as this would have been built around a central court that was open to the sky and large enough to enclose a garden with a fountain that served to both delight the eye and refresh the air. An arched entranceway to the house would have led into a large sitting room that occupied most of the ground floor.

An apartment such as the one that Nahray and his wife occupied would have been located above the ground floor, with rooms in the apartment laid out on two or more levels.

Off the living room there would have been several smaller rooms, including a kitchen, pantries for keeping perishable items cool, and a washroom lined entirely with marble.

On any given morning, Nahray would have left this comfortable abode to enter the teeming commercial world of Fustat to do business. Sometimes he might make his way to Fustat's Jewelry House, or Dar al-Jawhar, situated near the Mosque of 'Amr, one of the oldest mosques in the capital. Buyers and sellers from all over entered through the doors of the Dar al-Jawhar and engaged in a lively trade in gold necklaces, anklets, bracelets, and earrings; silver rings and pins; pearls; and semiprecious stones such as carnelian and lapis lazuli. Nahray would go there, for example, to assist Muslim merchants from Libya with the selling of beads.

As both the terminal and distribution center for goods passing to and from the Mediterranean and India, Fustat seemed never to sleep. Although Alexandria was the largest port in Egypt, commercially it ranked a distant second: All major transactions were made in Fustat-Cairo. Though Fustat's own port was hardly more than a pier where people and merchandise were disembarked, it could be reached directly by the shallow-draft boats traveling from the Mediterranean. Silk and copper came from Spain and Christian Europe, dried fruits from southwest Asia. Fustat itself refined and exported sugar. But textiles were far and away the main item of commerce, with Egyptian flax going to Tunisia and Sicily to return as finished fabrics. From head coverings to tunics, puffy-sleeved robes, scarfs, cloaks, and undergarments, the typical middle-class Cairene wardrobe fueled a hefty demand not only for local flax and wool but also for a wide variety of silks and linens from Tunisia, Spain, and Sicily.

By dealing in the textile trade, Nahray engaged in a pursuit traditionally dominated by Jewish merchants. But he also found himself trading in commodities as varied as Tunisian soap, Arabic books, North African felt, and a wide array of foodstuffs. Unloading his wares at the dock on a typical morning, Nahray might well have handled honey and olive oil from Tunisia; cheese from Sicily; and dried apricots, peaches, and plums from the eastern shores of the Mediterranean. Outgoing traffic was also heavy: Luscious Egyptian dates, for example, were coveted worldwide, and the wheat of Upper Egypt was renowned for its quality, both in Egypt and abroad.

Fustat-Cairo was the destination of innumerable ships coming up the Nile from the Mediterranean, a journey that was not without its risks. During the five- or six-day voyage between Fustat-Cairo and Alexandria, ships were often subject to attack. "We arrived safely, for God protected us from the bandits," one man wrote to his mother in Cairo, not hesitating to inform her that not everyone was so lucky. "A ship preceding us," he added, "was taken by them."

When robbers were not the problem, accidents were. To protect their goods against damage, merchants and ordinary citizens

A boat carrying turbaned Arab passengers and an apparently Indian crew sets sail for an Islamic port. Muslim merchants sailed to all parts of the known world, regularly crisscrossing the great seaborne trade routes, from the Mediterranean to the Indian Ocean to the China Sea.

alike used an ingeniously wide range of packing materials. Strong canvas was the most common wrapping, but other substances could serve as both disguise (for evading customs, perhaps) and padding. A package of mace, the spice made from nutmeg peel, might be placed inside a wickerwork basket full of ammonia salts, for example, or a package of silk buried in a consignment of wax. The name of the sender or receiver, or both, was then written on the outside of the parcel in red earth or indigo, often preceded by religious formulas such as "may God be its preserver" or "be it blessed." Because porters presumably could not read, merchants also used a variety of trademark designs. Nahray, for example, frequently marked his packages with the six-pointed Star of David.

Along with worries about the safety of his goods, Nahray also experienced considerable anxiety over the seasonal fluctuation in the level of the Nile. Reports of low water levels often inspired panic on the part of farmers for their summer crops, which needed the irrigation made possible by the river's annual floods. Food supply, prices, and the economy in general depended on this regular inundation. "The city is at a complete standstill," Nahray wrote to a business associate in Alexandria during the 1060s. "All the people's eyes are turned toward the Nile. May God in His mercy raise its waters." But while low water levels were a serious problem, too much water was just as dangerous. If too little water could result in famine, too much could lead to wholesale destruction. As one observer put it, the river was "the only [real] highwayman in Egypt, both desired and dreaded."

To carry the precious water where it was needed,

As recommended in penmanship manuals, a scribe writes while squatting, his paper resting on one knee. Arabic is written from right to left, without capitalization. The script is cursive and has either a rounded or angular shape, depending on the style used.

The Islamic Art of Calligraphy

No artists enjoyed higher status in the Islamic world than did calligraphers: The pen was said to be the first thing created by God, and the Arabic script was considered holy, the vehicle by which God gave man the Koran.

Professional scribes continued to produce copies of the Koran. But they also worked on a wide variety of other projects, such as drawing up government documents; copying books for libraries; and designing the inscriptions that adorned mosques, minarets, palaces, and tombs.

An aspiring calligrapher studied for years with a master to acquire such skill. Apprentices wrote out page after page of exercises, striving to create perfectly shaped and proportioned letters. Master and apprentice usually specialized in two or three of the six classic, rounded styles of Arabic writing; only the most proficient excelled at them all.

Apprentices also learned to make ink using indigo, henna, soot, and gum arabic. A master taught how to prepare paper by polishing it smooth with a stone, preferably agate, then ruling it with fine lines. The greatest secret he—or sometimes she—passed along was the technique for cutting a reed for the nib of a pen. So treasured was the pen that some calligraphers were buried with their best one; others bequeathed their favorites to the next generation of masters.

An inscription, rather than an image, identifies this playing card as the king of the polo-stick suit. Religious proscriptions against portraying living beings encouraged the use of calligraphy in art.

Many calligraphers protected their reed pens in metal boxes, though few would have been as elegant as the brass box at left. Circular containers held ink and sand for use as a blotting agent.

over the centuries the Egyptians had constructed an elaborate system of irrigation canals, and among the government's most sacred responsibilities was the maintenance of these waterways. There thus evolved annual rituals to open, or cut, the dirt dams that blocked the Nile-fed canals. An account of one such ceremony, just three years before Nahray's move to Egypt, describes the procession in which the young caliph al-Mustansir participated. At the head of the parade came trumpeters and drummers, followed by 10,000 men leading 10,000 horses with gold saddles and bridles inlaid with precious stones. After an interval came the caliph himself, mounted on a mule with an unadorned saddle and bridle and wearing a plain white linen caftan and turban. Behind him came various dignitaries, scholars, state officials, and visiting princes. As the caliph passed, bystanders lining the roadway prostrated themselves and called out blessings. Upon reaching the mouth of the canal, the caliph threw a spear at the dam, signaling the workmen to attack the barrier with their pickaxes, hoes, and shovels until the dam broke. And when the river's water flowed into the irrigation channels, the people felt reassured that their crops would prosper.

In addition to being essential to agriculture, the Nile was also the chief informal conduit for mail between Cairo and Alexandria. For both his private and business correspondence, Nahray would have relied not only on the professional overland mail—usually, but not always, regular and prompt—but also on colleagues, friends, and other travelers who regularly sailed between the two cities. "I am writing, after having dispatched to you several letters with Baruch," one of Nahray's relatives in Alexandria wrote to him, referring to a mutual friend. "I hope these have reached you."

Although Jewish, Nahray worked amicably with Muslims. Indeed, Muslim-Jewish

A Jewish child from Fustat-Cairo learned Hebrew by coloring in letters that a scribe had outlined in this 10th-century alphabet book. The book survived thanks to the medieval Jewish practice of preserving documents bearing God's name, a tradition sometimes extended to include anything written in Hebrew letters.

commercial partnerships were common in 11th-century Cairo, with Jewish businessmen often relying on Muslim agents and brokers, and vice versa. One Jewish silk-weaver's shop that employed Muslims and Jews was able to remain open on both Friday, the Islamic holy day, and Saturday, the Jewish Sabbath, since on either day at least some of the employees would be permitted to work. In another shop, the partners are said to have agreed that any profits made on Friday would go to the Jewish partners, and money earned on Saturday would go to the Muslim partners.

Being Jewish in an Islamic state carried with it certain restrictions. Nahray had to pay a yearly poll tax, for example, and was required at all times to carry a certificate proving that he had fulfilled this duty. But the Jewish community in Fustat-Cairo was

changed city. The ruling Fatimid dynasty was gone, and a new regime, the Mamluks, was in power. The portion of Fustat-Cairo that had once been restricted to residences for the elite of the Fatimid court had become a thriving commercial and residential center. And Cairo's population had soared to some 200,000 inhabitants, compared with roughly 80,000 in contemporary Paris and 60,000 in London; among all of the European cities, only Constantinople had a larger population.

Cairo boasted a number of impressive buildings. A massive hospital—divided into separate sections for men and women—treated as many as 4,000 patients a day, providing each overnight patient with a wooden bed, linens, a bedpan, and freshly laundered clothes. Not far away stood two great mosques, the al-Azhar and

"May God never separate you and me from our watans."

vibrant, and Nahray played an increasingly active role in it, for a time directing the affairs of two of Cairo's synagogues.

Clearly, after half a century, the erstwhile Tunisian immigrant had put down strong roots in his new homeland. This development was made clear by a wish expressed in a letter Nahray received late in his life from a cousin living in Cairo: "May God never separate you and me from our watans." The Arabic term had once designated the place where a man's family originated. In the world of Nahray's increasingly mobile Islamic society, however, *watan* had come to mean one's adopted city as well, a usage that in the case of Nahray ben Nissim was fitting indeed.

When Nahray's fellow Tunisian, Ibn Khaldun—the illustrious Islamic politician, historian, and jurist—arrived in Egypt some three centuries after Nahray's time, Fustat-Cairo was a much

the al-Hakim, along with ceremonial squares and the palaces and gardens of court functionaries. Even before he took up residence in Cairo, Ibn Khaldun declared of the city, "It is the mother of the world, the great center of Islam, and the mainspring of the sciences and the crafts."

Born in Tunis, which was by then independent of Egyptian rule, Ibn Khaldun had entered political and public life when he was still in his teens, serving in a variety of court capacities and surviving often perilous turns in the lives of his royal patrons. Thus, by the time he immigrated to Egypt in 1382, the 50-year-old Tunisian was largely inclined to retire from political service, even though he had gained considerable fame and influence as a statesman and historian. Despite this intention, Ibn Khaldun quickly came to the attention of the Mamluk ruler of Egypt, known as the sultan, the Arabic word for power; Sultan Barquq and Ibn Khaldun would form a friendship that lasted—with one major hiatus—for the rest of the sultan's life.

Soon after his arrival in Cairo, Ibn Khaldun was invited to deliver a series of lectures to an audience of scholars and court officials at the renowned al-Azhar mosque. Much impressed by Ibn Khaldun's learning and eloquence, Sultan Barquq appointed him in 1384 to teach jurisprudence at the Qamhiya Madrasa, a highly regarded college for the teaching of theology.

Though a recent immigrant, Ibn Khaldun not only occupied an enviable position among Cairo's intellectual elite but was also made responsible for the theological education of the broader Muslim community. According to Islamic custom, no one was to be excluded from seeking this higher learning. "To lock the door of a madrasa is to shut out the masses," wrote one scholar. "Let the door be opened and forbid no one of God's creatures to enter, just as if it were a mosque." Teaching at the madrasa was essentially oral and informal, taking place in rooms arranged around a courtyard. In the classic Islamic style, students might take dictation from the Koran, frequently committing large parts of the holy book to memory.

During this period, women as well as men were beginning to seek education, and among the Cairene women who entered the madrasa to study hadith, or Islamic tradition, was a truly extraordinary woman and scholar by the name of Umm Hani. Umm Hani's education in hadith was carefully supervised by her maternal grandfather and at least 13 other masters. In the course of her life, she bore seven children to two husbands, both of whom died. Upon her second husband's death, Umm Hani made use of her ample inheritance to buy an enormous spinning workshop and pursue her work as a teacher of hadith. Before her death in 1466, Umm Hani performed the pilgrimage to Mecca 13 times, often remaining there for months on end to teach.

About the same time that Umm Hani was embarking on her studies in hadith, Ibn Khaldun was gaining further honors under Sultan Barquq. In August of 1384, the same year as his inauguration as professor at the Qamhiya Madrasa, he was invested with the

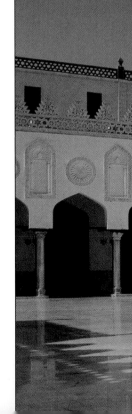

Above, a group of schoolboys recite verses of poetry for their cane-wielding teacher and an adult visitor to the school. After learning to write Arabic and memorizing the Koran, male students could proceed to an institution of higher learning, such as Cairo's al-Azhar mosque (right), which was home to two madrasas—colleges focusing on the study of Islamic law—and several teaching circles that formed around eminent scholars.

"robe of honor" of the qadi, or Islamic judge, and ascended to the position of chief qadi of the Malikites, which was one of the four schools of holy law.

During the elaborate investiture ceremony in the grand reception hall of the palace of the sultan, Barquq would have been dressed in a white turban and tunic, his usual attire during the hot Cairo summer. Ibn Khaldun would have worn the judge's robe of honor, a white woolen robe with green lining. Throughout the proceedings, Ibn Khaldun may have felt some pangs of regret that he was putting aside the pursuit of his scholarly interests and, as a major figure in the Mamluk administration of justice, being drawn into the public life he had hoped to abandon.

The Mamluks were a militaristic regime founded by former Turkish slaves trained from childhood for military service. They had ruled Egypt from the time of their successful coup d'etat in Cairo in 1250, and in 1260 had beaten back a Turkic advance toward Egypt at Ain Jalut in Palestine. In so doing, the triumphant Mamluk regime reaffirmed Egypt as the leading Muslim power and the center of what remained of Arabic culture. The regime was characterized by a rigorous hierarchy, extending from the lowest military and administrative levels all the way to the sultanate, the supreme power within the state. As in Ibn Khaldun's case, advancement and promotion depended almost entirely on gaining the sultan's favor.

Travelers on camels greet a villager in this illustration from a 13th-century Arab adventure book. Medieval Arab traders traveled throughout the world.

Traveling Afar

Muslims had been making long journeys since the first hajj to Mecca in the year 630. By the 1300s, Muslim envoys and traders, pilgrims and adventurers were traveling as never before, moving throughout a vast realm that extended from Spain and Morocco in the west to the island of Sumatra in the east.

Within the boundaries of this great swath of territory known as Dar al-Islam, the Realm of Islam, frontiers were abolished; commerce boomed; and adventurers, merchants, and shippers traveled with a freedom unknown since Roman times. One young Arab drawn to explore this world was a Moroccan legal scholar named Abu Abdallah ibn Battuta.

In 1325, at the age of 21, the Tangier native began his travels with the obligatory pilgrimage to Mecca. Ibn Battuta took a year and a half to reach the sacred city, however, visiting North Africa, Egypt, Palestine, and Syria along the way. Indeed, he would not return home for another quarter-century: After completing the hajj, he traveled to Iraq and Persia, then headed off to India—where he served as a qadi, or judge, for the sultan of Delhi—and eventually arrived in southern China.

Ibn Battuta was in his early 40s when he returned to his native land, where he wrote an account of his adventures. "I have," he declared, "attained my desire in this world, which was to travel through the earth." Ibn Battuta had crossed the entire Eurasian continent, logged 73,000 miles on the road, and visited the territories of 44 modern countries. In 1368 he died in the Moroccan capital, Fez, less than 150 miles from the place of his birth.

This map of the medieval world shows many of the lands visited by 14th-century Arab traveler Ibn Battuta. Not surprisingly, the Mediterranean, North Africa, and trade routes with China are more accurately depicted than are West Africa, western Europe, India, or Southeast Asia.

For the Mamluks, as for other Muslims, the sharia, or holy law, was comprehensive, defining the relations of men and women with God and with one another. Founded on the Koran, the traditions of the Prophet, and the logical deductions of legal scholars, its five-pointed scale of human actions—the obligatory, meritorious, indifferent, reprehensible, and forbidden—embraced all human activity. Within the sharia, four main schools of legal interpretation developed: the Hanafi, the Maliki, the Shafii, and the Hanbali. While the first three agreed on most important matters, the more traditionalist Hanbali opposed what it considered the speculative innovations of the other three schools.

Under the Mamluk regime, the four chief qadis made decisions mostly on points of religious law. In his new role as Malikite chief qadi, Ibn Khaldun would, like the other chief qadis, have been

did not typify Ibn Khaldun's approach to his new duties. Indeed, he entered into his role with a high degree of idealism, dedicated to protecting the common people of Cairo. He spurned, for example, the elaborate robes and turbans favored by the other qadis and continued to wear what he had worn back home in Tunisia, a one-piece hooded cloak known as a burnoose. Strictly refusing to participate in any form of corruption or bribery, he also declined honors and privileges that other qadis readily accepted. "I applied the Law of God with impartiality and without consideration of rank and power," Ibn Khaldun wrote, "putting the opposing parties always on the same footing, helping the weak to regain his rights, trying to learn the truth of the matter and rendering justice."

For many of his influential opponents, however, the manner in which Ibn Khaldun

"Is there any generosity left beyond that which you have already shown me?"

very concerned with the impact of law on the lives of ordinary citizens. Few descriptions of court cases of the day have survived, but one particular case does stand out. It involved a certain beautiful young woman who came before Hanafi chief qadi Husam al-Din al-Ghuri. Accompanied by her father, the woman complained that her husband was not living up to their marriage contract regarding her clothing and expense allowance, which was to be paid at the rate of one dinar per year. The judge, after ordering the woman to lower her veil so he could see her face, first yelled at the father for allowing his daughter to marry for so little money, and then proceeded to mock the husband as a fool. The wife, the judge proclaimed, was worth not one dinar a year but more than seven times that per night.

This rather profane example of the qadi's functions certainly

applied the law aroused bitter antagonism, particularly his attempts to reform influence peddling in the judicial arena. Those with whom he worked, such as secretaries and notaries, had other, more immediate, reasons for complaint, especially when he chose to punish them with what he called sticking—hitting with a spear until their necks were red. "Ibn Khaldun," wrote one colleague succinctly, "was exceedingly strict."

Certainly, matters of law and order in Sultan Barquq's Cairo were no laughing matter. For example, the festivities associated with Nawruz, the celebration of the vernal equinox, often erupted into violence and disorder. Appalled by the rowdiness of the citizens of Cairo, Barquq abolished the celebrations altogether in 1385. Officials then arrested those who tried to ignore the sultan's ruling, clubbing some of the revelers and cutting off the hands of others. The worst transgressors suffered even harsher punishment—death by hanging.

Less than a year after taking on the duties of chief qadi, Ibn Khaldun was mourning deaths in his own family. When he had immigrated to Egypt in 1382, he had left behind in Tunis a wife and five daughters. Deciding it was now time for them to join him, he persuaded Sultan Barquq to intervene on his behalf with the sultan of Tunis to allow the qadi's family to follow him to Cairo. Sufficiently flattered by Barquq's declaration that Ibn Khaldun had been "praising your Royal Highness since his arrival," the sultan of Tunis granted the request. But Ibn Khaldun's wife and daughters were not to be reunited with him. The ship carrying them to Egypt went down in a heavy storm, and they were drowned. Grief-stricken, Ibn Khaldun never really recovered from the loss. On June 17, 1385, still in despair and worn down by the relentless attacks of his opponents, he tendered his resignation from the judgeship.

Ibn Khaldun's public career was not over yet, however. After first appointing him teacher of hadith at another of Cairo's madrasas in late 1387, Sultan Barquq then chose

In the presence of two witnesses, the plaintiff in a legal dispute bows before the qadi, who wears a characteristic white head shawl over his turban. Instead of sitting in courtrooms, Cairo's lower-level judges heard cases in shops and market streets, by the city gates, and in other public spaces frequented by the common people.

Printing in the Islamic World

Printing in the medieval Islamic world was pioneered by an unlikely group: the Banu Sasan, a group of thieves, street urchins, and confidence men out to fleece the pious but gullible citizens of Cairo. To ward off evil and bring good luck, many Egyptians carried amulets bearing verses from the Koran, each laboriously copied by Muslim holy men. The Banu Sasan decided to mass-produce the verses and sell them as handwritten originals. In the process, they developed a method of printing unknown anywhere else except east Asia.

The men enlisted the services of an engraver, who used a sharp stylus to inscribe minute lines of the Koran on a wet clay tablet. The tablet was then baked in an oven or in the sun. After the clay tablet hardened, molten tin was poured into it, creating a plate with raised letters. Next, the tin plate was inked and pressed onto strips of paper two inches wide by six or so inches long. The strips were rolled up and put in tin or clay holders that could be worn on a cord around the neck.

Remarkably, the production of amulets by the Banu Sasan was the only known use of printing in medieval Islam. When the amulet trade ended in the 14th century—perhaps at the insistence of the religious establishment—so did printing in the Muslim world. It would not be seen again in the Middle East until a printing press was established in Istanbul in the early 18th century, this time introduced as an import from the West.

A member of the Banu Sasan appears before a Syrian governor in this 13th-century miniature. Despite their unsavory reputation, the Banu Sasan were popular at court as storytellers and entertainers.

Amulet scrolls like this one were mass-produced from woodblocks or tin plates and sold by Banu Sasan confidence men as one-of-a-kind, pen-and-ink originals. In addition to the tightly packed lines from the Koran, this particular amulet has been adorned with a decorative woodblock print.

Ibn Khaldun two years later to become overseer and controller of the Baybarsiya Khanqah, a Cairo hospice run by Sufi monks.

The Sufis practiced a somewhat different brand of religion from that of traditional Islam, mixing mysticism with more conventional Muslim beliefs. By this time, however, the Sufis played a key role in transmitting the message of Islam; their preaching was popular with the masses and reached into areas of the Muslim world that traditional scholars of the Koran could not. The Sufi hospices called *khanqahs* provided accommodations, meals, and cash stipends to Sufi mystics to support their work. The shaykh, the spiritual and scholarly head of the Sufi community, was a crucial link between the cloistered world of the khanqah and the common worshipers of Sufism. In principle, at least, there was no official recruitment of students: A shaykh might simply attract novices who, after his death, would carry on his teachings at the khanqah where he had lived. A disciple who placed himself in the hands of a shaykh had to obey at all costs, even if it meant subverting the law: He was to behave, as one authority put it, "like a corpse in the hands of the washer of the dead."

As witnessed by his appointment as director of the Baybarsiya Khanqah, Ibn Khaldun had continued to enjoy both the favor and support of the sultan, despite his resignation as chief qadi. All this changed in 1389, however, when Ibn Khaldun participated in a legal decision against his royal protector and benefactor. His action came after a group of rebels forced Barquq to relinquish his throne and then summoned Ibn Khaldun and a number of other officials to approve a legal decree, or fatwa, against the sultan. Perhaps under pressure from the rebel leaders, Ibn Khaldun signed the decree. Less than three months later, the rebellion was quashed, and the sultan returned to power. Angered by his former protégé's ingratitude, Barquq immediately dismissed Ibn Khaldun from his position at the Baybarsiya Khanqah.

Although not for the reason he would have chosen, Ibn Khaldun at last had his wish: He was now free to devote himself entirely to his scholarly pursuits and writing. This idyllic life lasted less than a decade. In May 1399 an apparently forgiving Sultan Barquq showed him favor once again, appointing him as Malikite chief qadi for a second time. Barquq died just one month later, but Barquq's young son, Faraj, the new sultan, confirmed his father's decision and retained Ibn Khaldun in his new position.

Faraj was not a strong ruler, however. Yielding to pressure exerted by certain officials critical of Ibn Khaldun, he dismissed the aging jurist from the judgeship in September 1400. Soon, though, Ibn Khaldun was given another, urgent mission by Sultan Faraj. Tamerlane, the great Turkic conqueror from central Asia (often, but erroneously, identified as a Mongol), had recently captured and destroyed the city of Aleppo; now he was poised to take Damascus and was even threatening Cairo. Faraj planned to travel to Syria to dissuade the invader, and since word of Ibn Khaldun's reputation had apparently reached Tamerlane, Ibn Khaldun would accompany the sultan and his royal party.

The plan went awry, however; Faraj, on learning of a threatened coup, effectively abandoned Ibn Khaldun in Syria to return to Cairo. Still, Ibn Khaldun was sure that he could negotiate the details of an armistice with Tamerlane, and in early January 1401 the 70-year-old diplomat reached Damascus. After greeting Turkic officials outside the city walls, he was led to Tamerlane's camp and then into the presence of the great leader, who, according to Ibn Khaldun, "was reclining on his elbow while platters of food were passed before him."

Ibn Khaldun spoke first, greeting Tamerlane with the words "peace be with you." Tamerlane raised his head, stretched out his hand for Ibn Khaldun to kiss as a show of respect, and gestured for him to sit. Some dishes of *rishta,* a kind of soup with macaroni, were then brought in. "Tamerlane made a sign that they should be set before me," Ibn Khaldun recalled later. "I arose, took them, and drank, and liked it, and this impressed him favorably."

Despite some language difficulties and the need to rely on an interpreter, the two men apparently communicated well. Indeed, Tamerlane must have been impressed with his visitor, for Ibn Khaldun remained in attendance with him and his council for more than a month. The unlikely pair discussed, among other issues, Ibn Khaldun's Maghrebi origins; the roles of Alexander the Great, Nebuchadnezzar, and other great historical figures; and predictions about the fate of the world's dynasties and empires.

At length Tamerlane asked Ibn Khaldun whether he would return to Cairo. Always prepared to take advantage of an opportunity, Ibn Khaldun seems to have answered somewhat ambiguously, "May Allah aid you! Indeed, my desire is only [to serve] you, for you have granted me refuge and protection. If the journey to Cairo would be in your service, surely! Otherwise, I have no desire for it." Tamerlane responded to this in no uncertain terms: "No, you will return to your family and to your people."

As he prepared to depart, Ibn Khaldun was overcome with emotion. "Is there any generosity left beyond that which you have already shown me?" he asked his host before leaving. "You have heaped favors upon me, accorded me a place in your council among your intimate followers, and shown me kindness and generosity—which I hope Allah will repay to you in like measures."

The arduous journey home across the desert roads of the Sinai Peninsula was not without peril, but Ibn Khaldun finally arrived in Cairo on March 17, 1401. It is not possible to know just how persuasive he was in securing an amnesty from Tamerlane for the citizens of Damascus, which soon fell to the invader; it is equally impossible to declare that Ibn Khaldun saved Cairo. But after Tamerlane captured Damascus, he and his army turned north toward Anatolia rather than south toward Egypt. Ibn Khaldun's adopted city continued to be, as he himself put it, "the metropolis of the universe, the garden of the world." Tamerlane's sense of Ibn Khaldun's rightful place had been an accurate one. As it was for Ibn Ridwan and as it became for Nahray ben Nissim, Cairo was now Ibn Khaldun's watan—his home.

Tamerlane of Samarkand

In the waning years of the 14th century, the Islamic world again faced invasion from central Asia. Like the Mongol forces of Genghis Khan almost 200 years before, great armies of mounted leather-clad warriors thundered southward, conquering, looting, and laying waste from Delhi to Damascus. Their leader, who claimed direct descent from the great khans but was in fact only a minor prince of Turkic descent, was named Timur, meaning iron. He was called Timur the Lame by his enemies and was later known in the West as Tamerlane.

Born in 1336 in Transoxiana, a region of central Asia that included the cities of Bukhara and Samarkand, Tamerlane dreamed of being a great warrior from early childhood. An arrow wound suffered in his mid-20s permanently injured his right leg, thus earning him his nickname, yet by age 34 he commanded a sizable army, had consolidated his power in his native region, and was poised to begin his planned conquest of the world. "As there is only one god in heaven," he proclaimed, "so should

A piercing gaze and stern visage characterize this bust of Tamerlane, which was fashioned by a Russian scientist who studied the warrior's skull after Tamerlane's remains were exhumed in the 1940s.

Domed mausoleums of the Shah-i-Zinda, or Shrine of the Living King, crown a hill above Samarkand. Tamerlane rebuilt the necropolis, a place of pilgrimage since the 11th century, as a royal cemetery for his family and friends.

Soldiers from Tamerlane's army besiege the ancient Persian city of Herat in this 15th-century miniature. After capturing Herat, they looted the city and carried its treasures, including a set of giant bronze doors, back to Samarkand.

there be only one monarch on earth."

Tamerlane first set his sights on neighboring Afghanistan and Persia, followed by portions of southern Russia and Iraq, including its capital of Baghdad. In 1398 Tamerlane's army of 90,000 warriors conquered much of India and destroyed ancient Delhi. Two years later Damascus and Tiflis, and a year after that most of Anatolia, fell to the fearsome man known as Earthshaker.

Everywhere the horde swept, death, destruction, and barbarity followed. In the town of Sabzawar in present-day Afghanistan, some 2,000 civilians were cemented alive into clay towers. At Delhi 100,000 Hindu prisoners were strangled in less than an hour, and a huge pyramid was created from their skulls. And at Smyrna, on the Aegean coast, Tamerlane's forces bombarded the escaping Christian fleet using severed heads as cannonballs.

Tamerlane's legendary cruelty toward his victims was equaled by his ambitious use of the plunder from his conquests. After each successful campaign, he rounded up the local architects and artisans and marched them, with their native materials and treasures, back to Transoxiana. There, astride the old Silk Road to China and near the remnants of the ancient city of Samarkand, he set about building his capital, a new Samarkand, which would soon become the finest city in central Asia and the "eye and star" of his empire.

Tamerlane waged his building campaign with the same zeal and speed that he devoted to his military operations. Like a phoenix rising from the ashes, Samarkand grew from a small city to a metropolis of 150,000 people in less than

Aided by captured elephants, Indian artisans wrestle with giant building stones during the construction of the massive Bibi Khanum mosque. The mosque, named for Tamerlane's favorite wife, took five years to complete, with the ruler urging on the builders with coins and scraps of meat.

The Bibi Khanum's turquoise dome rests on an earth-toned drum faced with glazed mosaics that spell out verses from the Koran. When completed in 1404, the mosque was the largest and most beautiful in central Asia. A court chronicler wrote of the structure, "Its dome would have been unique had it not been for the heavens, and unique would have been its portal had it not been for the Milky Way." Its hasty construction, however, resulted in its ruin over the next few centuries.

35 years. Ornate palaces, graceful formal gardens, bustling bazaars, and imposing blue-tiled mosques, madrasas, and mausoleums sprang up. There was a constant flurry of activity as captured Indian elephants dragged huge building blocks here and there, and stonemasons, tile glaziers, silk weavers, and other craftsmen from all the vanquished lands labored mightily to bestow their talents on their adopted city. Around the periphery of Samarkand lay a ring of villages that Tamerlane derisively named after the workers' former homelands—Baghdad, Damascus, Shiraz, and Delhi.

During most of the frenzied construction of Samarkand, Tamerlane was off waging his many campaigns. But in 1404 he returned home for a rare four-month stay. His purpose was to plan a major invasion of China, but he also utilized the respite for a succession of festivals and other fetes, including the weddings of his 11-year-old grandson and five other princes. Among the hundreds of guests was Spanish emissary Ruy González de Clavijo, whose vivid recollections offer a lasting portrait of Tamerlane, his court, and his glorious "Blue City."

"We found Timur seated under a portal before a most beautiful palace," González de Clavijo recounted. "He was lounging against some pillows upon a raised dais before which there was a fountain where red apples floated. He was dressed in a cloak of plain silk, and he wore a tall white hat on the crown of which was displayed a balas ruby, and was further ornamented with pearls and precious stones." González de Clavijo went on to

Reposing in a canopied pavilion while musicians and dancers entertain and attendants bring food and drink, Tamerlane receives his infant son Shah Rukh in 1377. An avid chess player, he had named the child the Persian word for check during a successful game.

The fluted dome of Tamerlane's mausoleum, the Gur-i-Amir, rises above the ruler's jade tombstone, which bears the inscription, "If I were alive today, mankind would tremble!"

describe the intelligence and graciousness of his host, the beauty and dress of Tamerlane's wives, and the abundance of fine food and drink. Though Tamerlane was a devout Muslim, his faith did not extend to the avoidance of alcohol.

In January 1405, against all advice, Tamerlane embarked on what was to be his final campaign. Even though he had assembled the largest army in history, he could not defeat winter or his own age and infirmities. Still far from China, he developed pneumonia and died. So as not to unsettle the troops, his perfumed body was placed in a bejeweled coffin and dispatched in the dead of night for burial in his beloved Samarkand.

Tamerlane's legacy to the lands he had conquered was not one of empire. He brought temporary order to a politically chaotic period in the Islamic world, but he could not make it last beyond his own lifetime. Culturally, however, his legacy was rich. The arts, especially intricate tile work and miniature painting, flourished under his successors, as did the science of astronomy. And beautiful Samarkand became not only the economic and cultural capital of central Asia but its scientific and artistic heart as well.

Flanked by three madrasas, or Islamic schools, Samarkand's Registan has been called central Asia's most noble public space. In Tamerlane's day the square served as the city's main bazaar and site of declarations of war, public executions, and displays of spiked heads and loot from victorious campaigns.

GLOSSARY

Abbasid: the second Islamic dynasty, whose caliphs traced their descent from Muhammad's uncle al-Abbas and who ruled the Muslim world from their principal capital of Baghdad from 750 to 1258.

Adab: a genre of Arabic literature that seeks to teach good manners in a light, elegant style and often employs animal characters.

AH: meaning "After Hijra," a notation used with dates to indicate the year of the Muslim lunar calendar, which is calculated from the time of Muhammad's Hijra, or emigration, to Medina in 622.

Al-Andalus: Arabic name for Spain, used as early as 716; lands under Muslim rule on the Iberian Peninsula between the seventh and 13th centuries.

Allah: literally, "the one God." The God of Islam.

Amir: literally, "prince." The title of a Muslim military commander or provincial governor.

Astrolabe: instrument of Muslim invention, predating the sextant, used to calculate the altitude of the sun and other celestial bodies.

Baraka: spiritual power or grace inherent in a holy person or object; it is a source of blessing.

Bedouins: tribal pastoral nomads indigenous to the deserts of Arabia.

Berbers: tribal nomads native to North Africa who initially resisted but eventually converted to Islam between the ninth and 12th centuries; they helped spread Islam to sub-Saharan Africa.

Caftan: long-sleeved, ankle-length robe, customarily worn in Middle Eastern and Mediterranean societies.

Cairene: resident of Cairo, Egypt.

Caliph: from the Arabic word *khalifa,* meaning "successor" or "follower"; a ruler who succeeded the prophet Muhammad as supreme Muslim leader and who had both political and religious authority.

Caliphate: the position and authority of the Islamic caliph, successor to Muhammad as supreme leader of the Muslim world.

Caravan: a company of travelers and their pack animals journeying together, particularly across a desert.

Companions: Muhammad's closest associates; they were among the first converts to Islam.

Dar: literally, "house" or "abode."

Dar al-Islam: the "abode" of Islam; lands where Islam is the established religion.

Dinar: Muslim gold coin.

Dirham: Muslim silver coin.

Fatimid: dynasty of caliphs, claiming descent from Muhammad's daughter Fatima, who ruled North Africa and Egypt from Cairo from 909 to 1171.

Fatwa: authoritative opinion on a point of Islamic law given by a mufti, or learned legal expert.

Fennec: small fox with large pointed ears, native to the deserts of North Africa.

Fitna: dissension or civil war; in particular, the first Muslim civil war, which followed the murder of the third caliph, Uthman, in 656; from the Arabic word for "temptation," referring to the temptation to settle disputes by force of arms.

Hadith: literally, "narrative" or "talk." Collective body of traditions relating to the life, actions, and sayings of Muhammad; second only to the Koran as a source of Islamic law and dogma.

Hajib: literally, "doorkeeper." The official chamberlain who regulated access to a Muslim ruler.

Hajj: annual pilgrimage to Mecca that every Muslim is obliged to make at least once in their lives.

Harem: private quarters in a home reserved for the women of the family; unrelated adult males are not allowed access.

Harisa: a Middle Eastern dish of ground meat and wheat fried in fat, similar to hamburger.

Harras: the chef-vendor who prepares and sells the ground meat and wheat dish called harisa.

Henna: a reddish dye used as a cosmetic and obtained from the leaves of the henna plant, which is indigenous to North Africa and Asia.

Hijab: screen or veil that shields a Muslim woman from public view. The word was originally used in reference to the curtain that Muhammad hung in his home to seclude the women of his family; it later also came to mean veil.

Hijaz: the northwest part of the Arabian Peninsula, including the cities of Mecca and Medina, celebrated as the birthplace of Islam.

Hijra: forced emigration of Muhammad and his followers in 622 from Mecca to Medina, where they established the first Muslim-governed society.

Hilm: skillful manipulation of others using tact, cunning, patience, and the threat of coercion.

Howdah: a seat, often fitted with a canopy and railing, placed on the back of an elephant or camel.

Humors: the four fluids—blood, phlegm, yellow bile, and black bile—formerly believed to be responsible for human health, as first postulated by ancient Greek physicians.

Ibn: literally, "son." Used in Arabic names to link the name of the individual with that of his father; alternative forms include bin, ben, and—for daughters—bint.

Imam: prayer leader; honorific title given a Muslim scholar; supreme head of the Shiite Muslim community.

Infidel: nonbeliever; one without faith, especially in a specific religion, in particular Islam or Christianity.

Islam: literally, "submission" or "surrender." One of the three great religions—along with Judaism and Christianity—that profess belief in a single, all-powerful God. Islam arose among the Arabs in the seventh century and spread within a century to North Africa, to Spain, and eastward across Asia as far as the borders of China.

Ismailis: secretive missionary sect of Shiite Muslims that was first organized in the mid-eighth century and gave rise to the Fatimid dynasty that ruled North Africa and Egypt from 909 to 1171.

Jihad: Arabic for "struggle" or "strife." A struggle against inner weakness; a Muslim holy war against infidels, or nonbelievers.

Jinns: genies; legendary supernatural beings who, in the pagan tradition of pre-Muslim Arabs, dwell on the earth, assume the shapes of wild animals and snakes, inspire humans to create poetry, and may inflict harm—often in the form of death or madness—on those who offend them.

Kaaba: Islam's most venerated shrine; the cube-shaped building at the center of the Great Mosque at Mecca, where Muslims believe Abraham built the first house of worship to the one God.

Katib: government secretary or clerk.

Khanqah: a Sufi hospice, similar to a monastery and often dedicated to charitable and missionary work, where a particular shaykh might live and teach his disciples.

Kharijite: literally, "secessionist." Sect of Muslims, formerly Shiite, who insisted that the caliph, or supreme Muslim leader, be elected on the basis of demonstrated piety and moral character and should be deposed by force, if necessary, if he abused his moral authority while in office.

Kohl: a powdery black cosmetic used as eye makeup.

Koran: from the Arabic *qur'an,* meaning "revelation" or "recitation." The holy scripture of Islam, consisting of the revelations transmitted by God to Muhammad through the angel Gabriel.

Madrasa: literally, "place of study." A college, frequently attached to a mosque, that specializes primarily but not exclusively in the teaching of Islamic law.

Maghreb: literally, "the West." The Islamic West, which included North Africa and Spain.

Mamluk: literally, "slave" or "owned." Slave-soldiers of Asian origin who served Abbasid caliphs; the militaristic dynasty founded by Mamluk warriors that ruled Egypt, Syria, and Arabia from 1250 to 1517.

Maqama: (pl. maqamat) a genre of Arabic literature in which a medley of rhymed prose and verse relates a dramatic anecdote; style is emphasized rather than content.

Maqsura: screened area in an Islamic place of worship reserved for the caliph or his representative.

Mihna: inquisition; ordeal, misfortune; in particular, the 12-year religious inquisition begun by the caliph al-Mamun shortly before his death in 833.

Mihrab: niche in an Islamic place of worship indicating the qibla, or direction of Mecca.

Minaret: from the Arabic word *manara,* meaning "place of light"; tall tower attached to a mosque from which the Muslim faithful are called to prayer.

Mosque: place where Muslims gather to worship.

Muallaqat: a collection of Arabic literature consisting of seven celebrated odes; the word means "suspended poems," and they were legendarily hung in the Kaaba, or sacred shrine, at Mecca.

Muezzin: crier who calls the Muslim faithful to prayer five times daily.

Mufti: expert in Islamic law and custom who people consult for authoritative legal opinions.

Musk: powerfully fragrant substance secreted by certain animals, used in perfumery.

Muslim: from the Arabic for "one who surrenders"; a follower of Islam.

Nawruz: a week-long spring festival, formerly in celebration of the Persian New Year (at the vernal equinox) but adopted by Muslims as a secular holiday, during which people perfume their houses, exchange gifts, and rejoice in the streets.

Necropolis: cemetery, especially of an ancient city.

Oasis: a fertile place in a desert, suitable for agriculture and permanent settlement because of the presence of water.

Pillars of Islam: the five main requirements of Islam: daily worship, fasting, almsgiving, confession of faith, and pilgrimage to Mecca.

Primogeniture: being the firstborn or eldest child; the right of the firstborn to inherit his parents' entire estate.

Prophet: one who speaks by divine inspiration; one through whom the will of a god is expressed.

Qadi: Muslim judge who rules especially on points of religious law.

Qasida: ode; a genre of early northern Arabian poetry originally presented by reciters and consisting of rich metrical rhyming verse.

Qataif: Middle Eastern sweetmeat made with flour and almonds.

Qibla: direction to which Muslims turn in prayer, toward Mecca.

Ramadan: the ninth month of the Muslim lunar year, during which Muslims abstain from eating or drinking from sunrise to sunset.

Rishta: a Mongolian soup containing macaroni.

Sadaq: a midwinter festival of Persian origin, adopted by Muslims as a secular holiday, during which celebrants light bonfires and fumigate their homes to ward off misfortune; also known as "the night of fires."

Salat: formal Islamic prayer undertaken five times daily during which Muslims turn toward Mecca, prostrate themselves, and worship Allah, the one God.

Saracens: common term for Muslims in medieval Europe.

Sharia: the corpus of supreme Muslim law, based on the Koran and hadith, or Islamic tradition; the entirety of the Islamic way of life.

Shaykh: literally, "old man." Tribal chief; religious leader; spiritual and teaching head of a Sufi community.

Shia: literally, "faction." Sect of Muslims who rejected the historical succession of caliphs and insisted that only Ali, cousin of Muhammad and husband of Muhammad's daughter Fatima, and Ali's descendants could rightfully succeed Muhammad. Shiite Muslims also tended to emphasize the caliph's religious rather than political authority.

Shura: literally, "committee" or "council." The committee of six electors appointed by the second Islamic caliph, Umar, to choose his successor.

Sufis: Muslim mystics, also known as "friends of God," who sought union with God through the teachings and rituals of individual shaykhs and who preached the message of Islam to the masses, in both Muslim and non-Muslim societies; from the Arabic *suf,* or wool, in reference to the coarse woolen cloaks worn by Sufis.

Sufism: Islamic mysticism centered on the teachings of individual shaykhs; it became popular, in the form of organized brotherhoods, throughout the Islamic world from the 12th century.

Sultan: a political title first granted by caliphs in the 11th century to independent local Muslim rulers. Originally bestowed on individuals, the title was by the 13th century assumed as a prerogative by some local dynasties and was the title assumed by the Mamluks who ruled Egypt, Syria, and Arabia from 1250 to 1517.

Sunni: from the Arabic *sunna,* meaning "the path" or the "way of Muhammad"; orthodox sect of Muslims that accepted the historical succession of caliphs and tended to emphasize the caliph's political rather than religious authority.

Suq: literally, "market." Usually refers to the

main commercial district of an Islamic town or city.

Sura: chapter of the Koran, the holy scripture of Islam.

Tiraz: from the Persian *taraz,* meaning adornment; silk embroidered fabrics made in state workshops and distributed as gifts by a Muslim ruler; the inscriptions on such fabrics.

Turban: headdress worn by Muslim men, consisting of a length of fabric wound in folds about the head.

Ud: stringed musical instrument, the Arab forerunner of the European lute.

Umayyad: the first Islamic dynasty, founded by the fourth caliph Muawiya in 661, which ruled from Damascus until 750. When the Umayyads were overthrown by the Abbasids in 750, the sole surviving member of the Umayyad ruling family fled to Spain and founded a new branch of the dynasty, which ruled there from 756 to 1031.

Ushnan: pulverized ashes of alkaloid plants, used as soap.

Venesection: the cutting of a vein; the practice of bloodletting as a therapeutic measure.

Vizier: literally, "minister." Under the Abbasid caliphs, the vizier was prime minister; later the term denoted lower officials.

Watan: literally, "place of birth" or "homeland."

PRONUNCIATION GUIDE

Abbasid (ab-BA-sihd)
Abd al-Malik (abd el-MA-lik)
Abd al-Rahman (abd el-rah-MAN)
Abu Talib (a-boo TAW-lib)
Adab (a-dab)
Aisha (A-ee-sheh)
Al-Amin (el-a-MEEN)
Al-Andalus (el-AN-da-loos)
Al-Azhar (el-AZ-har)
Alhambra (el-HAM-bra)
Al-Mansuriyya (el-man-soo-REE-ya)
Al-Muizz (el-moo-IZ)
Amir (a-MEER)
Banu Sasan (ba-noo sa-SAN)
Baraka (BA-ra-ka)
Caliph al-Mansur (KAY-lif el-man-SOOR)
Dirham (DEER-ham)
Fatima (FAH-ti-ma)
Fatimid (FAH-ti-mid)
Fatwa (FEHT-wa)
Hadith (ha-DEETH)
Harun al-Rashid (ha-ROON el-ra-SHEED)
Hashimites (HA-shi-mites)
Hijab (heh-JAHB)
Hijaz (hi-JAZ)
Hijra (HIJ-ra)
Ibn Khaldun (ibn khahl-DOON)

Ibn Ridwan (ibn rid-WAHN)
Imam (ee-MAM)
Ishmael (ISH-mah-el)
Islam (is-LAHM)
Ismaili (is-ma-EE-lee)
Jihad (ji-HAD)
Kaaba (KAH-ba)
Kairouan (keye-ra-wan)
Khadija (kha-DEE-ja)
Khalifa (kha-LEE-fa)
Khurasan (khu-rah-SAHN)
Koran (koh-RAHN)
Kufa (KOO-fa)
Madinat al-Zahra (meh-DEE-nat el-ZAH-ra)
Madrasa (MEH-dreh-seh)
Maghreb (MAG-rib)
Mamluk (mam-LOOK)
Mamun (ma-MOON)
Maqamat (ma-KAW-MAT)
Maqsura (mak-SOO-ra)
Medina (meh-DEE-na)
Mihna (MIH-na)
Muallaqat (moo-al-la-KAHT)
Muawiya (moo-AH-wee-ya)
Muezzin (moo-EH-zin)
Muhammad (moo-HAM-mad)
Muthanna (moo-THAN-na)

Nahray ben Nissim (nah-RAY ben nee-SEEM)
Nawruz (now-rooz)
Qadi (KAH-dee)
Qasidah (ka-SEE-da)
Qibla (KIB-la)
Ramadan (rah-mah-DAHN)
Salat (sah-LAHT)
Sharia (sha-REE-a)
Shaykh (SHAY-kh)
Shia (SHEE-a)
Shiite (SHEE-ite)
Shura (SHOO-rah)
Sultan (sool-TAHN)
Suq (sook)
Sura (SOO-ra)
Taif (TAH-ehf)
Tiraz (tee-RAHZ)
Ud (ood)
Umayyad (oo-MEYE-yad)
Uqba ibn Nafi (OOK-ba ibn NA-fee)
Vizier (vi-ZEER)
Watan (WAH-tan)
Yazid (ya-ZEED)
Ziryab (zeer-YAB)
Ziyad (zee-YAD)
Zubayda (zoo-BEYE-da)

ACKNOWLEDGMENTS AND PICTURE CREDITS

ACKNOWLEDGMENTS

The editors wish to thank the following individuals and institutions for their valuable assistance in the preparation of this volume:

Tayeb El-Hibri, Amherst, Mass.; John Esposito, Georgetown University, Washington, D.C.; Heinz Gruber, Österreichische Nationalbibliothek, Vienna; Mary Ison and Staff, Library of Congress, Washington, D.C.; Heidrun Klein, Bildarchiv Preussischer Kulturbesitz, Berlin.

BIBLIOGRAPHY

BOOKS

Abbott, Nabia. *Two Queens of Baghdad: Mother and Wife of Harun al-Rashid.* Chicago: University of Chicago Press, 1946.

Ahsan, Muhammad Manazir. *Social Life under the Abbasids: 170-289 AH, 786-902 AD.* London: Longman, 1979.

Al-Andalus: The Art of Islamic Spain. Ed. by Jerrilynn D. Dodds. New York: Metropolitan Museum of Art, 1992.

al-Maqqari, Ahmad ibn Muhammad. *The History of the Mohammedan Dynasties in Spain,* Vol. 2. Trans. and ed. by Pascual de Gayangos. New York: Johnson Reprint, 1964.

And, Metin. *Istanbul in the 16th Century: The City, the Palace, Daily Life.* Istanbul: Akbank, 1994.

Arabesques et Jardins de Paradis: Collections Françaises d'Art Islamique. Paris: Éditions de la Réunion, 1989.

Arabian Peninsula. Alexandria, Va.: Time-Life Books, 1986.

Armstrong, Karen. *Muhammad: A Biography of the Prophet.* San Francisco: HarperCollins, 1992.

Atil, Esin. *Renaissance of Islam: Art of the Mamluks.* Washington, D.C.: Smithsonian Institution Press, 1981.

Badeau, John S., et al. *The Genius of Arab Civilization.* New York: New York University Press, 1975.

Baker, Patricia L. *Islamic Textiles.* London: British Museum Press, 1995.

Baladhuri, Ahmad ibn-Jabir. *The Origins of the Islamic State.* Trans. by Philip Khuri Hitti. Beirut: Khayats, 1966 (reprint of 1916 edition).

Barrucand, Marianne, and Achim Bednorz. *Moorish Architecture in Andalusia.* Cologne: Taschen, 1992.

Berkey, Jonathan. *The Transmission of Knowledge in Medieval Cairo: A Social History of Islamic Education.* Princeton, N.J.: Princeton University Press, 1992.

Bloom, Jonathan M. "The Origins of Fatimid Art." In *Muqarnas: An Annual on Islamic Art and Architecture,* Vol. 3. Ed. by Oleg Grabar. Leiden, Netherlands: E. J. Brill, 1985.

Bloom, Jonathan, and Sheila Blair. *Islamic Arts.* London: Phaidon, 1997.

Blunt, Wilfrid. *The Golden Road to Samarkand.* New York: Viking Press, 1973.

Bonavia, Judy. *The Silk Road: From Xi'an to Kashgar.* Kowloon, Hong Kong: Odyssey, 1999.

Brend, Barbara. *Islamic Art.* Cambridge, Mass.: Harvard University Press, 1991.

Bulliet, Richard W.:
  The Camel and the Wheel. Cambridge, Mass.: Harvard University Press, 1975.
  Islam: The View from the Edge. New York: Columbia University Press, 1994.

Bulliet, Richard W., et al. *The Earth and Its Peoples: A Global History.* Boston: Houghton Mifflin, 1997.

The Cambridge Illustrated History of the Islamic World. Ed. by Francis Robinson. Cambridge: Cambridge University Press, 1996.

Chejne, Anwar G. *Muslim Spain: Its History and Culture.* Minneapolis: University of Minnesota Press, 1974.

Child, John. *The Rise of Islam.* New York: Peter Bedrick Books, 1992.

Christians and Moors in Spain, Vol. 1. Wiltshire, England: Aris & Phillips, 1993.

Cleary, Thomas. *The Essential Koran: The Heart of Islam.* San Francisco: HarperCollins, 1993.

Cohen, Mark R. *Jewish Self-Government in Medieval Egypt.* Princeton, N.J.: Princeton University Press, 1980.

Constable, Olivia Remie. *Trade and Traders in Muslim Spain.* Cambridge: Cambridge University Press, 1994.

Cook, Michael. *Muhammad.* Oxford: Oxford University Press, 1983.

Creswell, K. A. C. *The Muslim Architecture of Egypt: Ayyubids and Early Bahrite Mamluks, A.D. 1171-1326,* Vol. 2. New York: Hacker Art Books, 1978.

De Carthage à Kairouan: 2000 Ans d'Art et d'Histoire en Tunisie. Paris: Musée du Petit Palais de la Ville de Paris, 1983.

Denny, Frederick M. *Islam and the Muslim Community.* San Francisco: HarperCollins, 1987.

Donner, Fred McGraw. *The Early Islamic Conquests.* Princeton, N.J.: Princeton University Press, 1981.

Dunn, Ross E. *The Adventures of Ibn Battuta: A Muslim Traveler of the 14th Century.* Berkeley: University of California Press, 1986.

El-Hibri, Tayeb. *Reinterpreting Islamic Historiography: Harun al-Rashid and the Narrative of the Abbasid Caliphate.* New York: Cambridge University Press, 1999.

The Encyclopaedia of Islam, Vols. 1-10. Leiden, Netherlands: E. J. Brill, 1960-98.

Escovitz, Joseph H. *The Office of Qâdî al-Qudât in Cairo under the Bahrî Mamlûks.* Berlin: Klaus Schwarz, 1984.

Esposito, John L. *Islam: The Straight Path.* New York: Oxford University Press, 1991.

Ettinghausen, Richard:
  Arab Painting (Treasures of Asia series). Geneva: Skira, 1962.
  "Further Comments on Mamluk Playing Cards." In *Gatherings in Honor of Dorothy E. Miner.* Ed. by Ursula E. McCracken, Lilian M. C. Randall, Richard H. Randall, Jr. Baltimore: Walters Art Gallery, 1974.

Fernandes, Leonor. *The Evolution of a Sufi Insti-*

tution in Mamluk Egypt: The Khanqah. Berlin: Klaus Schwarz Verlag, 1988.

Fernández-Puertas, Antonio. *The Alhambra, Vol. 1: From the Ninth Century to Yusuf I (1354).* London: Saqi, 1997.

Fischel, Walter J.:
Ibn Khaldun and Tamerlane. Berkeley: University of California Press, 1952.
Ibn Khaldun in Egypt. Berkeley: University of California Press, 1967.

Fletcher, Richard. *Moorish Spain.* New York: Henry Holt and Co., 1992.

Gabrieli, Francesco. *Muhammad and the Conquests of Islam.* Trans. by Virginia Luling and Rosamund Linell. New York: McGraw-Hill Book Co., 1968.

Gibb, H. A. R. *Arabic Literature.* Oxford: Clarendon Press, 1963.

Gippenreiter, Vadim E. *Fabled Cities of Central Asia: Samarkand, Bukhara, Khiva.* New York: Abbeville Press, 1989.

Glory of Byzantium: Art and Culture of the Middle Byzantine Era, A.D. 843-1261. Ed. by Helen C. Davis and William D. Wixom. New York: Metropolitan Museum of Art, 1997.

Glubb, John Bagot. *The Great Arab Conquests.* New York: Barnes & Noble, 1995.

Goitein, S. D. *A Mediterranean Society:*
Economic Foundations, Vol. 1. Berkeley: University of California Press, 1967.
The Community, Vol. 2. Berkeley: University of California Press, 1971.
The Family, Vol. 3. Berkeley: University of California Press, 1978.
Daily Life, Vol. 4. Berkeley: University of California Press, 1983.
The Individual, Vol. 5. Berkeley: University of California Press, 1988.

Goitein, S. D., trans. *Letters of Medieval Jewish Traders.* Princeton, N.J.: Princeton University Press, 1973.

González de Clavijo, Ruy. *Narrative of the Embassy of Ruy González de Clavijo to the Court of Timour at Samarcand, A.D. 1403-6.* Trans. by Clements R. Markham. New York: Lenox Hill, 1970 (reprint of 1859 edition).

Grabar, Oleg:
The Alhambra. Sebastopol, Calif.: Solipsist Press, 1992.
The Formation of Islamic Art. New Haven: Yale University Press, 1987.

The Illustrations of the Maqamat. Chicago: University of Chicago Press, 1984.

Grube, Ernst J. *The World of Islam.* New York: McGraw-Hill Book Co., 1967.

Grube, Ernst J., et al. *Architecture of the Islamic World.* Ed. by George Mitchell. London: Thames and Hudson, 1978.

Gutas, Dimitri. *Greek Thought, Arabic Culture.* London: Routledge, 1998.

Guthrie, Shirley. *Arab Social Life in the Middle Ages.* London: Saqi Books, 1995.

Halm, Heinz:
The Empire of the Mahdi: The Rise of the Fatimids. Trans. by Michael Bonner. New York: E. J. Brill, 1996.
The Fatimids and Their Traditions of Learning. London: Institute of Ismaili Studies, 1997.

Hariri. *Makamat.* Trans. by Theodore Preston. London: Darf, 1986.

Hassan, Ahmad Yusuf. *Islamic Technology.* Cambridge: Cambridge University Press, 1986.

Hawting, G. R. *The First Dynasty of Islam: The Umayyad Caliphate, AD 661-750.* Carbondale: Southern Illinois University Press, 1987.

Hillenbrand, Robert. *Islamic Architecture: Form, Function and Meaning.* New York: Columbia University Press, 1994.

Horizon History of Africa. New York: American Heritage, 1971.

Hourani, Albert. *A History of the Arab Peoples.* Cambridge, Mass.: Belknap Press, 1991.

Howell, Anthony. *Imruil: A Naturalized Version of His Ode-Book.* London: Barrie & Jenkins, 1970.

Ibn Batuta. *The Travels of Ibn Batuta.* Trans. by Samuel Lee. New York: Johnson Reprint, 1968 (reprint of 1829 edition).

Ibn Hisham, Abd al-Malik. *The Life of Muhammad: A Translation of Ishaq's Sirat Rasul Allah.* New York: Oxford University Press, 1997.

Ibn Jubayr. *The Travels of Ibn Jubayr.* Trans. by R. J. C. Broadhurst. London: Jonathan Cape, 1952.

Ibn Ridwan, 'Ali. *Medieval Islamic Medicine.* Trans. by Michael W. Dols. Berkeley: University of California Press, 1984.

Irving, Thomas Ballantine. *Kalilah and Dimnah.* Newark, Del.: Juan de la Cuesta, 1980.

Irwin, Robert. *Islamic Art in Context: Art, Architecture, and the Literary World.* New York: Harry N. Abrams, 1997.

Islamic Calligraphy: Sacred and Secular Writings. Geneva: Musée d'art et d'histoire, 1988.

James, David. *Qur'ans of the Mamluks.* New York: Thames and Hudson, 1988.

Jazari, Ibn al-Razzaz. *The Book of Knowledge of Ingenious Mechanical Devices.* Trans. by Donald R. Hill. Dordrecht, Holland: D. Reidel, 1974.

Jenkins, Marilyn. *Islamic Glass: A Brief History.* New York: Metropolitan Museum of Art, 1986.

Jewish World: History and Culture of the Jewish People. New York: Harry N. Abrams, 1979.

Johnson, Gordon. *Cultural Atlas of India.* New York: Facts On File, 1996.

Jomier, Jacques. *How to Understand Islam.* New York: Crossroad, 1989.

Kay, Shirley. *This Changing World: The Bedouin.* New York: Crane, Russak & Co., 1978.

Kennedy, Hugh:
The Early Abbasid Caliphate. London: Croom Helm, 1981.
Muslim Spain and Portugal: A Political History of al-Andalus. London: Longman, 1996.

King, John. *Karakoram Highway: The High Road to China.* Berkeley, Calif.: Lonely Planet, 1989.

Lapidus, Ira Marvin:
A History of Islamic Societies. Cambridge: Cambridge University Press, 1988.
Muslim Cities in the Later Middle Ages. Cambridge, Mass.: Harvard University Press, 1967.

Lassner, Jacob. *The Topography of Baghdad in the Early Middle Ages.* Detroit: Wayne State University Press, 1970.

Lawton, John. *Samarkand and Bukhara.* London: Tauris Parke Books, 1991.

Legacy of Muslim Spain. Ed. by Salma Khadra Jayyusi. New York: E. J. Brill, 1992.

Lévi-Provençal, E.:
Histoire de L'Espagne Musulmane, Vol. 3. Paris: Éditions G.-P. Maisonneuve & Cie, 1953.
L'Espagne Musulmane au Xéme Siécle. Paris: Larose, 1932.

Lewis, Bernard, et al.:
Islam and the Arab World: Faith, People, Culture. New York: Alfred A. Knopf, 1976.
The Middle East: A Brief History of the Last 2,000 Years. New York: Touchstone, 1995.
The World of Islam: Faith, People, Culture. London: Thames and Hudson, 1976.

Lings, Martin. *Muhammad: His Life Based on the Earliest Sources.* New York: Inner Traditions International, 1983.

MacLeod, Calum, and Bradley Mayhew.

Uzbekistan: The Golden Road to Samarkand. Hong Kong: Odyssey, 1997.

Manz, Beatrice Forbes. *The Rise and Rule of Tamerlane.* Cambridge: Cambridge University Press, 1989.

March of Islam: TimeFrame AD 600-800. Alexandria, Va.: Time-Life Books, 1988.

Mayer, L. A.:
Mamluk Costume. Genève: Albert Kundig, 1952.
Mamluk Playing Cards. Leiden, Netherlands: E. J. Brill, 1971.

Mez, Adam. *The Renaissance of Islam.* Trans. by Salahuddin Khuda Bukhsh and D. S. Margoliouth. New York: AMS Press, 1975 (reprint of 1937 edition).

Minbar from the Kutubiyya Mosque. New York: Metropolitan Museum of Art, 1998.

Moktefi, Mokhtar. *The Rise of Islam.* Trans. by Nan Buranelli. Morristown, N.J.: Silver Burdett Press, 1986.

Morony, Michael G. *Iraq after the Muslim Conquest.* Princeton, N.J.: Princeton University Press, 1984.

Nasr, Seyyed Hossein. *Islamic Science: An Illustrated Study.* [s.l.]: World of Islam Festival, 1976.

Nicholson, Reynold A. *A Literary History of the Arabs.* Surrey, England: Curzon Press, 1993 (reprint of 1907 edition).

Norwich, John Julius. *Byzantium: The Apogee.* New York: Alfred A. Knopf, 1997.

Oxford Illustrated History of the Crusades. Ed. by Jonathan Riley-Smith. Oxford: Oxford University Press, 1995.

Petry, Carl F. *The Civilian Elite of Cairo in the Later Middle Ages.* Princeton, N.J.: Princeton University Press, 1981.

Prussin, Labelle. *Hatumere: Islamic Design in West Africa.* Berkeley: University of California Press, 1986.

Rahman, H. U. *A Chronology of Islamic History, 570-1000 CE.* Boston: G. K. Hall & Co., 1989.

Random House Dictionary of the English Language. New York: Random House, 1987.

Raymond, André. *Le Caire.* Paris: Fayard, 1993.

Riley-Smith, Jonathan, ed. *The Atlas of the Crusades.* New York: Facts On File, 1991.

Rogers, Michael. *The Spread of Islam.* Oxford: Elsevier-Phaidon, 1976.

Rubin, Uri. *The Eye of the Beholder: The Life of Muhammad as Viewed by the Early Muslims.* Princeton, N.J.: Darwin Press, 1995.

Russell, Dorothea. *Medieval Cairo and the Monasteries of the Wadi Natrun.* London: Weidenfeld and Nicolson, 1962.

Sanders, Paula. *Ritual, Politics, and the City in Fatimid Cairo.* Albany: State University of New York Press, 1994.

Saunders, J. J. *A History of Medieval Islam.* London: Routledge, 1996.

Schacht, Joseph, and Max Meyerhof. *The Medico-Philosophical Controversy between Ibn Butlan of Baghdad and Ibn Ridwan of Cairo.* Cairo: Egyptian University, 1937.

Schimmel, Annemarie. *Calligraphy and Islamic Culture.* New York: New York University Press, 1984.

Shanks, Hershel. *Jerusalem: An Archaeological Biography.* New York: Random House, 1995.

Shoshan, Boaz. *Popular Culture in Medieval Cairo.* Cambridge: Cambridge University Press, 1993.

Sicily: Insight Guides. Ed. by Lisa Gerard-Sharp. London: APA, 1996.

Smith, Bradley. *Spain: A History in Art.* Garden City, New York: Doubleday & Co., 1971.

Spellberg, D. A. *Politics, Gender, and the Islamic Past: The Legacy of A'isha bint Abi Bakr.* New York: Columbia University Press, 1994.

Splendours of an Islamic World. London: Tauris Parke Books, 1997.

Staffa, Susan Jane. *Conquest and Fusion: The Social Evolution of Cairo, A.D. 642-1850.* Leiden, Netherlands: E. J. Brill, 1977.

Stewart, Desmond. *The Alhambra.* New York: Newsweek, 1974.

Stewart, Desmond, and the Editors of Time-Life Books. *Early Islam* (Great Ages of Man series). New York, N.Y.: Time-Life Books, 1967.

Stierlin, Henri. *Islam, Vol. 1: Early Architecture from Baghdad to Cordoba.* Cologne: Taschen, 1996.

Stone-Ferrier, Linda A. *Dutch Prints of Daily Life: Mirrors of Life or Masks of Morals?* Lawrence, Kans.: Spencer Museum of Art, 1983.

Stowasser, Karl. "Manners and Customs at the Mamluk Court." In *Muqarnas: An Annual on Islamic Art and Architecture,* Vol. 2. Ed. by Oleg Grabar. New Haven, Conn.: Yale University Press, 1984.

Tabari:
The Crisis of the Early Caliphate. Vol. 15 of *The History of al-Tabari.* Trans. by R. Stephen Humphreys, ed. by Ehsan Yar-Shater. Albany: State University of New York Press, 1990.
The Reunification of the Abbasid Caliphate. Vol. 32 of *The History of al-Tabari.* Trans. by C. E. Bosworth, ed. by Ehsan Yar-Shater. Albany: State University of New York Press, 1987.

Terzioglu, Derin. "The Imperial Circumcision Festival of 1582: An Interpretation." In *Muqarnas: An Annual on Islamic Art and Architecture,* Vol. 12. Ed. by Gülru Necipoglu. Leiden, Netherlands: E. J. Brill, 1995.

Treadgold, Warren. *The Byzantine Revival, 780-842.* Stanford, Calif.: Stanford University Press, 1988.

Treasures of Islam. London: Philip Wilson, 1985.

Trésors Fatimides du Caire. Paris: Institut du Monde Arabe, 1998.

Udovitch, A. L. "A Tale of Two Cities." In *The Medieval City.* Ed. by Harry A. Miskimin, David Herlihy, and A. L. Udovitch. New Haven, Conn.: Yale University Press, 1977.

Waines, David. *In a Caliph's Kitchen.* London: Riad El-Rayyes Books, 1989.

Watt, W. Montgomery:
Muhammad at Mecca. Oxford: Clarendon Press, 1953.
Muhammad at Medina. Oxford: Clarendon Press, 1956.

Welch, Anthony. *Calligraphy in the Arts of the Muslim World.* Austin: University of Texas Press, 1979.

Wellhausen, Julius:
The Arab Kingdom and Its Fall. Trans. by Margaret Graham Weir, ed. by A. H. Harley. London: Curzon Press, 1973.
The Religio-Political Factions in Early Islam. Trans. by R. C. Ostle and S. M. Walzer, ed. by R. C. Ostle. Amsterdam: North-Holland, 1975.

Wepman, Dennis. *Tamerlane.* New York: Chelsea House, 1987.

PERIODICALS

El-Hibri, Tayeb. "Harun al-Rashid and the Mecca Protocol of 802." *International Journal of Middle East Studies,* August 1992.

Lev, Yaacov. "Army, Regime, and Society in Fatimid Egypt, 358-487/968-1094." *International Journal of Middle East Studies,* August 1987.

Udovitch, A. L. "Merchants and Amirs: Government and Trade in Eleventh-Century Egypt." *Asian and African Studies,* November 1988.

INDEX

Numerals in italics indicate an illustration of the subject mentioned.

TIME LIFE BOOKS

Time-Life Books is a division of Time Life Inc.

TIME LIFE INC.
PRESIDENT and CEO: Jim Nelson

TIME-LIFE BOOKS
PUBLISHER/MANAGING EDITOR: Neil Kagan
SENIOR VICE PRESIDENT, MARKETING:
Joseph A. Kuna
VICE PRESIDENT, NEW PRODUCT
DEVELOPMENT: Amy Golden

What Life Was Like ®
IN THE LANDS OF THE PROPHET

EDITOR: Denise Dersin
Deputy Editor: Paula York-Soderlund
Art Director: Alan Pitts
Text Editor: Robin Currie
Associate Editor/Research and Writing: Trudy W. Pearson
Copyeditors: Leanne Sullivan (principal),
Mary Beth Oelkers-Keegan (senior)
Technical Art Specialist: John Drummond
Editorial Assistant: Christine Higgins
Photo Coordinator: David Herod

Special Contributors: Ronald H. Bailey, Michael Blumenthal, Ellen Galford (chapter text); Jane Coughran, Stacy W. Hoffhaus, Christina Huth, Jane Martin, Elizabeth Thompson, Roger Williams, Barry N. Wolverton (research-writing); Meghan K. Blute, Sarah L. Evans, Rena Kakani, Miriam Simon (research); Constance Buchanan, Roberta Conlan (editing); Barbara L. Klein (overread); Barbara Cohen (index).

Correspondents: Christine Hinze (London), Christina Lieberman (New York), Maria Vincenza Aloisi (Paris); valuable assistance also provided by Elisabeth Kraemer-Singh, Angelika Lemmer (Bonn), Caroline Wood (London)

Separations by the Time-Life Imaging Department

NEW PRODUCT DEVELOPMENT:
Director, Elizabeth D. Ward; Project Manager, Barbara M. Sheppard; Director of Marketing, Mary Ann Donaghy; Marketing Manager, Paul Fontaine; Associate Marketing Manager, Erin Gaskins

MARKETING: Director, Pamela R. Farrell; Marketing Manager, Nancy Gallo; Associate Marketing Manager, Erin Trefrey

Executive Vice President, Operations: Ralph Cuomo
Senior Vice President and CFO: Claudia Goldberg
Senior Vice President, Law & Business Affairs: Randolph H. Elkins
Vice President, Financial Planning & Analysis: Christopher Hearing

Vice President, Book Production: Patricia Pascale
Vice President, Imaging: Marjann Caldwell
Director, Publishing Technology: Betsi McGrath
Director, Editorial Administration: Barbara Levitt
Director, Photography and Research: John Conrad Weiser
Director, Quality Assurance: James King
Manager, Technical Services: Anne Topp
Senior Production Manager: Ken Sabol
Manager, Copyedit/Page Makeup: Debby Tait
Production Manager: Virginia Reardon
Chief Librarian: Louise D. Forstall

Consultant:

Richard W. Bulliet was educated at Harvard University and is currently a professor of history at Columbia University. He also serves as director of Columbia's Middle East Institute. Dr. Bulliet's research has concentrated on the social history of the Islamic community and on the history of technology. He has published extensively, most recently as co-author of a college history textbook, *The Earth and Its Peoples: A Global History,* as co-editor of *The Encyclopedia of the Modern Middle East,* and as editor of *The Columbia History of the Twentieth Century.*

First printing. Printed in U.S.A.
School and library distribution by Time-Life Education, P.O. Box 85026, Richmond, Virginia 23285-5026.

TIME-LIFE is a trademark of Time Warner Inc. and affiliated companies.

Library of Congress Cataloging-in-Publication Data
What life was like in the lands of the Prophet : Islamic world, AD 570-1405 / by the editors of Time-Life Books.
         p.   cm.—(What life was like ; 16)
     Includes bibliographical references (p. -) and index.
     ISBN 0-7835-5465-6
     1. Civilization, Islamic.   2. Islamic Empire—Social life and customs.   3. Islamic Empire—Social conditions.   I. Time-Life Books.   II. Title: In the lands of the Prophet.   III. Series: What life was like series ; 16.
DS36.855.W48   1999   99-37865
909'.097671'01—dc21   CIP
10 9 8 7 6 5 4 3 2 1
For information on and a full description of any of the Time-Life Books series listed, please call 1-800-621-7026 or write:
Reader Information, Time-Life Customer Service,
P.O. Box C-32068, Richmond, Virginia 23261-2068

Other Publications:
HISTORY
Our American Century
World War II
The American Story
Voices of the Civil War
The American Indians
Lost Civilizations
Mysteries of the Unknown
Time Frame
The Civil War
Cultural Atlas

COOKING
Weight Watchers® Smart Choice Recipe Collection
Great Taste~Low Fat
Williams-Sonoma Kitchen Library

SCIENCE/NATURE
Voyage Through the Universe

DO IT YOURSELF
Custom Woodworking
Golf Digest Total Golf
How to Fix It
The Time-Life Complete Gardener
Home Repair and Improvement
The Art of Woodworking

TIME-LIFE KIDS
Student Library
Library of First Questions and Answers
A Child's First Library of Learning
I Love Math
Nature Company Discoveries
Understanding Science & Nature

This volume is one in a series on world history that uses contemporary art, artifacts, and personal accounts to create an intimate portrait of daily life in the past.